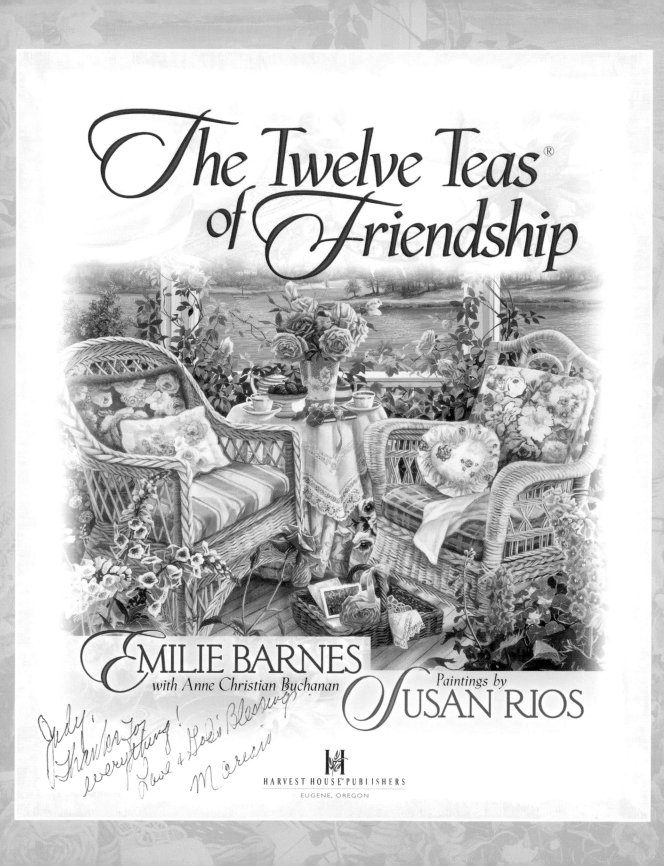

The Twelve Teas® of Friendship

EMILIE BARNES

with Anne Christian Buchanan

Paintings by
SUSAN RIOS

Judy,
Thanks for
everything!
Love & God's Blessings
Marcia

HARVEST HOUSE PUBLISHERS

EUGENE, OREGON

The Twelve Teas® of Friendship

Text copyright © 2001 by Emilie Barnes and Anne Christian Buchanan
Published by Harvest House Publishers
Eugene, Oregon 97402
www.harvesthousepublishers.com

Library of Congress Cataloging-in-Publication Data

Barnes, Emilie.
  The twelve teas of friendship / Emilie Barnes, with Anne Christian Buchanan ; painting by Susan Rios.
     p. cm.
  ISBN 0-7369-0474-3
   1. Afternoon teas. 2. Tea. 3. Friendship. I. Buchanan, Anne Christian. II. Title.

TX736 .B375 2001
641.5'3--dc21

2001020416

THE TWELVE TEAS® is a registered trademark of The Hawkins Children's LLC. Harvest House Publishers, Inc. is the exclusive licensee of the federally registered trademark of THE TWELVE TEAS®.

Original Artwork © Susan Rios. Licensed by Art Impressions, Canoga Park, CA.
For more information regarding artwork featured in this book, please contact:

> Art Impressions
> 9035-A Eton Avenue
> Canoga Park, CA 91304-1616
> (818) 700-8541

Design and production by Garborg Design Works, Minneapolis, Minnesota

Harvest House Publishers, Inc. is the exclusive licensee of the trademark THE TWELVE TEAS.

Scripture quotations are from the Holy Bible: New International Version ®. NIV ®. Copyright © 1973, 1978, 1984 by the International Bible Society. Used by permission of Zondervan Publishing House.

Printed in Hong Kong

04 05 06 07 08 09 10 /NG/ 10 9 8 7 6

CONTENTS

Introduction
A CELEBRATION OF SISTERHOOD

Through the seasons, through the years, it's your friends who carry you through. What would you do without them—these chosen sisters who laugh with you, cry with you, and speak truth to you? And what better way to celebrate the warmth and intimacy of beautiful friendship than with the warmest and most intimate of celebrations—a tea.

That's the reason for this book. It's a collection of seasonal celebrations for you to share with the friends you love—new friends and old, fun friends and friends in need, big groups of friends and intimate gatherings. Most of all, it's a book of celebration. It's a book to help you celebrate—in your heart and in your home—the special friends who love and support you, who teach you and learn from you, who bring a special brightness to your good years and literally save you in your tough times.

What do you *do* with these friends at a tea party?

Well, for one thing, you drink tea. But anyone who has enjoyed a childhood tea party knows you can hold a lovely tea without the tea. Fruit juice, hot chocolate, or even warm milk will serve just as well. You can even hold a tea party with iced tea.

There's food, of course. A well-appointed tea table might feature luscious warm scones with clotted cream, or elegant puff pastry with caviar, or even, in the case of the traditional British high tea, a full meal. However varied the fare, there's something about a warm cup of tea that brings out the best of savory or sweet.

There are other things you can do at a tea. A tea is really a party, after all, which opens the door to all sorts of possibilities. You can play games, for instance—icebreaker games, games of wit and words. If you play bridge or hearts, in fact, the game might be the very purpose for the tea.

You can also enjoy entertainment at your teas. Music at tea is traditional, whether it comes from a CD player in the background or a string quartet hired for the occasion. And you'd be very much in the teatime tradition to enjoy a small homegrown entertainment together afterward—a song around the piano, a short story read aloud, or even a mutually loved "chick flick."

There's so much you can do to enhance your enjoyment of the special times you spend with friends new and old. But don't think you have to fill every minute with activities. What you're there for is each other. You're there to talk and to listen and to enjoy the relationship-enhancing ritual of gathering around a beautiful table, of pouring tea for each other, of sharing delicious food, of being both formal and warm with one another.

The Twelve Teas of Friendship, in other words, is as much about friendship as it is about tea. Although it's full of easy recipes, doable decorating tips, and fun ideas, its primary intention is to remind you just how precious your friendships are and how important it is to nurture them in a variety of ways—including the sharing of tea.

Through the seasons, through the years, the time to gather with your friends for tea is anytime at all. May you continue to carry each other through as you celebrate the beautiful gift of your life together.

January
CELEBRATING NEW FRIENDS AND OLD

A Gold-and-Silver Tea

Make new friends and keep the old,
One is silver and the other gold.
—Old Rhyme

A new year, a fresh start—with all those lovely unused days and fresh opportunities stretched out before you. And though you never really know what the coming year will bring, don't you always hope it brings new friends?

A fun and delicious way to help the process along is to host a "share your friends" tea. Planned around a theme of silver and gold—for new friends and old—it's the kind of celebration that's guaranteed to bring warmth and discovery to your most blustery winter day.

This idea works best if you

invite a group of women you know casually but not intimately. They can be coworkers, the mothers of your children's friends, people you've met at church, the spouses of your husband's colleagues—anyone you enjoy and would like to get to know better. But the fun really starts when you ask each guest to bring *another* friend—preferably someone you don't know. If you invite six people, you'll have a party full of twelve potential friends. To make the whole thing even more fun, ask one of your closest friends to host the party with you.

Although tea parties don't always require invitations, this is an occasion where an invitation can be very helpful. These can be as formal or informal as you like, as long as you explain the concept clearly and include your phone number so you'll know who is going to attend. The invitations will be extra special if you write or print them in gold or silver ink (see page 10 for an easy but effective invitation idea).

Name tags are also optional for a tea but especially helpful for this "get to know you"

party. Here's a novel twist on the name tag idea that can serve as an icebreaker and help with your decor: Simply gather an assortment of small, inexpensive, gold and silver photo frames from your local closeout store. As each guest arrives, snap her picture with a Polaroid or a digital camera, write her name below her face with a permanent marker, and pop the photo in a frame. Arrange the photos on a sideboard or your tea table and urge the guests to use them as a reference for matching names to faces.

A Welcoming Setting

Decorating for your gold-and-silver tea is fun and easy, especially if you take advantage of the after-Christmas sales. Look for metallic-trimmed linens and dishes to grace your tea table, tiny silver and gold balls to spark your flower arrangements, metallic ribbon to serve as napkin rings—whatever catches your eye. Then, to warm up the color scheme and take away the Christmasy feel, add the gold and silver accents to an underlying palette of lovely peaches and corals.

You can make a beautiful and unusual centerpiece by filling several glass containers of different sizes with little gold and silver glass balls or glass pebbles, then arranging flowers and greenery in the vases. (Check your local supermarket for fragrant coral roses, peach-colored carnations, or even pale salmon orchids.) Grouping the containers together on a silver platter or small mirror will add a sense of unity and a beautiful sparkle. Place a few containers of matching flowers around the house—and decorate the door with a bouquet tied in silver-and-gold ribbon.

Table linens can be silver or gold, a coral color to match the flowers, or snowy white. If your tablecloth doesn't have metallic accents, you can add some by crisscrossing the cloth with gold-and-silver ribbon, letting the pieces hang gracefully down the sides. The same ribbon, tied around each napkin, becomes a festive napkin ring—and why not add a matching bow to the teddy bear in the corner, the concrete goose on the doorstep, or the group of iron tools by the fireplace?

A silver tea service, if you own or can borrow one, is a lovely traditional way to carry out the silver-and-gold theme, and metallic gold paper doilies arranged on silver platters present your delicious tea food to beautiful advantage. But don't despair if you don't have any real silver or gold or gold-rimmed bone china teacups! Hospitality and friendship can glimmer in *any* setting. You can put together a delightful gold-and-silver tea with metal-toned plastic trays from the craft store and a set of gold-and-silver paper plates. The real silver and gold at this particular tea party will be the new friends and old who gather under your roof.

$\mathcal{S}$OMETHING $\mathcal{D}$ELICIOUS

Serve a good-quality black tea at your gold-and-silver tea, accompanied with milk and lump sugar—and a generous spread of dainty delights. Try the recipes shown here or your own favorites.

A PERFECT POT OF TEA
Although friends and fellowship are the central purpose for any tea party—and this one in particular—

the star performer on any tea table is the tea itself. Here are a few tips on brewing a truly delightful six-to eight-cup pot of tea.

> Good-quality loose tea (use 1 teaspoon of loose tea per cup plus one spoonful "for the pot") or tea bags (1 bag less than the number of cups you desire)
> Boiling water
> Milk, sugar, honey, or lemon, as desired

Begin by filling a teakettle with freshly drawn cold water and putting it on to boil. While the kettle is heating, pour hot water into a ceramic or glass teapot to warm it. (Brewing tea in metal pots may impart a metallic taste. It's fine, however, to transfer the tea to a metal container once it's brewed.) When the pot has had time to warm, pour out the hot water and add the tea, then put the lid back on the pot until the water boils. As soon as the kettle comes to a rolling boil, remove from heat—don't overboil. Pour boiling water into the teapot and let the tea brew from three to six minutes. Lengthening the brewing time will just make the tea taste bitter—if you want stronger tea, use more tea leaves, not more time.

Gently stir the tea before pouring it through a tea strainer into the teacups. (If you used tea bags, remove them.) Serve with cream (really milk), sugar, honey, or lemon. If your guests take milk, pour it into the cup first, then add the tea.

SPICED HONEY STARS

These delicious little cookies are daintily spiced with a hint of orange—warm flavors for a cold day. This recipe makes about 5 dozen cookies.

> 1/2 cup butter, softened
> 3/4 cup sugar
> 1 egg
> 1/4 cup honey
> grated peel of one small orange
> 2 cups flour
> 1 teaspoon baking soda
> 1 teaspoon cinnamon
> 1/2 teaspoon ground ginger
> 1/4 teaspoon ground cloves
> Royal Icing (recipe below) and silver baking
>   ornaments

Preheat oven to 375°. Cream butter and sugar together thoroughly, then add eggs, honey, and orange peel and beat until smooth. Sift together flour, soda, and spices, then stir into butter mixture. Turn dough out onto well-floured surface (dough will be soft) and roll to 1/8-inch thickness. Cut out cookies with a 2-inch star-shaped cutter.

Bake on ungreased cookie sheet for 7–8 minutes. Let stand for a few minutes before removing to wire racks to cool. Decorate as desired with Royal Icing and little silver candies.

ROYAL ICING

> 2 teaspoons powdered egg whites
>   (meringue powder)
> 2 2/3 cups confectioners' sugar
> 1/4 cup water

Combine all ingredients and beat with electric mixer for 8–10 minutes, until peaks form and icing is the texture of sour cream. Thin icing with water a drop at a time until about consistency of honey. For each star, place a blob of icing in the center and use a knife tip or chopstick to push the thin icing into a star shape on top of the cookie, leaving edges brown. Let icing harden before serving or storing cookies.

Something to Make
A Gracious Invitation

Here's an easy and elegant homemade invitation that can adapt itself to a number of occasions. For each invitation, you'll need a heavy sheet of 8½ x 11-inch paper. You'll also need a pencil, scissors or a craft knife, gold and silver paint pens with a medium or wide point, a fine-point pen in blue or black, and a small piece of cardboard to make a template. If you want to mail the invitations, you'll need to purchase envelopes large enough to hold a 4¼ x 5½-inch card.

To make the invitation, fold the sheet of paper in half, bringing the short edges together, then fold in half again. You should now have a folded 4¼ x 5½-inch card. Position it so that it opens like a book in front of you—with open edges at right and bottom. Mark the front or top surface of the card very lightly with a pencil. Open up the paper, which is now marked by the folds into rectangles, and look for the rectangle you marked. Using the pattern on page 11, trace an oval shape onto cardboard, cut it out to make a template, then center it on the front rectangle and trace around it. Carefully cut out this oval with scissors or a craft knife, then refold the card so that the front has an oval "window." With a pencil, lightly trace around the window onto the next layer of paper. Then use the silver and gold paint pens to draw a wavy "picture frame" around the oval, alternating scalloped silver and gold lines until the "frame" is about ½-inch thick. Outline the frame with the blue or black fine-tip pen and draw in alternating silver and gold lines behind the frame to suggest striped wallpaper. If you wish, add lines at top to suggest an old-fashioned wire picture hanger.

Open out the card once more and find the oval you penciled in. Place the cardboard template over it, matching the edges to the penciled lines, and trace around the template with a black

Make new friends and keep the old, One is silver and the other gold.

–Old Rhyme

or blue fine point pen. Use the same pen to write the little "silver and gold" poem found at the beginning of this chapter. When you refold the card once more, the poem should appear in the frame. Then open the card like a book and write your actual invitation inside:

PLEASE COME TO A
GOLD-AND-SILVER TEA
ON FRIDAY, JANUARY 12
AT 5:15 IN THE EVENING.

HELP US ALL EXPAND OUR CIRCLE
OF FRIENDS
BY BRINGING A GUEST THE REST OF US MIGHT
NOT KNOW.

RSVP 691-7881 (EMILIE) OR 584-1243 (ANNE)
(PLEASE HELP US PREPARE BY LETTING US KNOW
THE NAME OF THE PERSON YOU PLAN TO BRING.)

Teatime Tidbits

THERE ARE REALLY ONLY THREE KINDS OF TEA—ROBUST *BLACK TEAS*, MADE FROM LEAVES THAT HAVE BEEN ALLOWED TO FERMENT; DELICATE *GREEN TEAS*, WHICH ARE STEAMED INSTEAD OF FERMENTED; AND IN-BETWEEN *OOLONG TEAS*, WHICH ARE ONLY PARTIALLY FERMENTED. ANY OF THESE THREE BASIC VARIETIES CAN BE BLENDED, SCENTED, OR FLAVORED WITH FRUIT, FLOWERS, OR HERBS. BUT A TRUE "HERBAL TEA" IS NOT REALLY A TEA AT ALL BECAUSE IT CONTAINS NO TEA LEAVES!

For Your Table
A CLEAR WINNER

Teatime is the occasion to enjoy your most beautiful cups, saucers, plates, and platters as well as your treasured china or silver tea service. But if you don't happen to own a matched set, don't let that deprive you of the pleasures of tea. Begin with what you have, borrow what you can, give out notice among your friends and family about what you would like in the future. In the meantime, I suggest investing in a simple white ceramic pot, a creamer and sugar bowl, and an inexpensive set of white or clear glass dishes from a discount or department store. You'll need cups, saucers, and small luncheon or dessert plates to serve at least six—and a couple of platters will come in handy. The beauty of this simple set is its versatility—you can transform your tea table simply by changing the linens or employing one of several creative decorating tricks. Then, as you acquire more expensive items, the basic pieces will still supplement your tea things beautifully. There'll always be a place on any tea table for crystal-clear or pure white beauty.

Something to Think About
THE ART OF FINDING FRIENDS

"If you want to have friends, be friendly." That's great advice as far as it goes, but sometimes the process of friend-finding could use a bit of a jump start. Here are some practical ideas for striking the friendship spark.

- *Carry a card.* Keep a small supply of business or calling cards in your purse so it's easy to say, "Call me."
- *Drop a line.* If you meet someone you'd like to know better, drop her a note—or get on your computer and send a friendly e-mail.
- *Issue an invitation.* When you meet someone new and interesting, invite her to go for a walk, have lunch with you—or come to tea!
- *Take notes.* Write down important things you learn about a new acquaintance—her birthday, family's names, and so on. Your friendship will grow faster if you're not always having to cover new ground.
- *Offer a welcome.* If someone new moves into

your neighborhood or church, take a minute for an old-fashioned gesture of welcome—a basket of local information and coupons, a home-baked treat, or even a store-bought pie.

- *Open your mind.* Your next best friend just might be someone you don't expect—older, younger, or simply different.

- *Leave room in your life for future friends.* Try scheduling some things to do alone—a daily walk, a stroll through a museum—with the idea that you might share that time later with a new friend.

- *Learn something new.* Take a class, join a study group, start a new hobby. The more you ask questions and participate in your new interest, the more potential friends you're apt to meet.

- *Nourish spiritual connections.* Keep your eyes open as you attend worship or other religious activities. If you meet someone who seems to share your spiritual interests, ask if she would consider sharing or praying with you on a regular basis.

- *Ask for help with a project.* It's not only a good way to get the job done; it's a nice way to get to know someone better.

- *Offer someone a ride to a meeting or other gathering.* The gesture is usually appreciated, and the commute is a nice time to get to know each other better.

- *Keep a "yes" in your heart.* You never know whether the next person you meet will turn out to be a dear chosen sister.

One of the best gifts you can give to a friend is to share your other friends.

13

February
CELEBRATING COZY RELATIONSHIPS

A "Just for Us" Tea

"Friendship," said Christopher
Robin, *"is a very comforting
sort of thing to have."*
—A. A. Milne

What is more comforting on a gloomy February morning than a cup of hot tea, a cozy-bozy flannel robe, and the nearness of a dear friend?

You can celebrate that special coziness by inviting two or three of your nearest and dearest for a snuggly teatime. Invite them on a Saturday morning for a teatime brunch—maybe after a "just us girls" sleepover—or on a blustery Sunday afternoon.

You don't need to restrict yourself to the dining room or living room for this special cozy tea. Seek out the most comfortable room in the house—the kitchen, the family room, a light-filled sunroom—even your bedroom. For a really creative twist, serve tea on bed trays on a big pillow-filled bed.

Ask everyone to wear their comfiest clothes—even robes and jammies. This isn't a formal, good-manners tea, though of course you *always* want to treat your friends with special courtesy. Concentrate on warmth and comfort—and make sure your special guests know they can stay as long as they like; they're part of the family. You might even want to greet each guest at the door with a new pair of deliciously warm bedroom slippers—or bring them into the kitchen to help you cook. (There's more time to talk if you're making the goodies together!)

This is the perfect kind of tea to precede or follow an indoor afternoon together. When you're through, wash the dishes together, then settle down to a craft project or a great old movie or manicures and pedicures for everyone or a special time of prayer. Before you know it, you might find yourselves pulling the tea things out once again—for yet another warm teatime.

An Intimate Setting

Set the stage for this coziest of all tea parties by covering your table with oh-so-soft flannel. A sheet will work nicely, or you can buy some yardage from a fabric store and cut it to size with pinking shears. For an especially adorable setting, try making a tablecloth and matching napkins from white flannel sprigged with pink rosebuds, then top the tablecloth with a 36-inch square tea cloth in a matching solid pink. (If you want to serve this tea on trays, just cut pieces of flannel with pinking shears to fit the tray.)

Decorate your table and your rooms with dainty porcelain mugs and pitchers that pick up the colors of your flannel. You can even use an extra teapot for a vase. Fill the pots and pitchers with ivy and simple, inexpensive flowers such as daisies or baby carnations.

Don't forget to carry your coziness theme throughout the rooms of your house. Be sure there are plenty of fluffy pillows and warm quilts available. You can even tuck your regular sofa pillows into flannel pillowcases. Perch a couple of squishy, huggable teddy bears on extra chairs or benches. Set out lots of family photos and pictures of your guests as well. And if you have a fireplace, by all means have it lit and burning—a reminder that the home fires are always burning for your special friends.

SOMETHING DELICIOUS

JAM TEA

This is the kind of sweet specialty we all enjoyed as children. Why not share it with your friends?

> 1 pot hot English Breakfast tea
> 1 teaspoon jam per cup of tea—try raspberry, strawberry, apricot, or even mint
> sugar to taste
> whipped cream (optional)

Place 1 teaspoon jam in the bottom of a cup. Pour the hot tea over the jam and stir. Add sugar and top with whipped cream if desired.

IRISH OATMEAL SCONES

Scones don't have to look like biscuits or wedges. This easy variation came from a farmhouse in Ireland. Enjoy with sweet jam and imitation clotted cream. This recipe will make 12 muffin-shaped scones.

> nonstick cooking spray
> ¾ cup milk or cream
> 1 large egg
> 3–4 tablespoons light brown sugar

1 teaspoon vanilla
2 ¼ cups all-purpose flour
1 cup old-fashioned rolled oats
1 tablespoon double-acting baking powder
½ teaspoon baking soda
½ teaspoon salt
¾ stick (6 tablespoons) cold unsalted butter, cut into bits
½ cup currants

Spray a 12-cup muffin pan with nonstick spray and set aside. In a bowl, whisk together milk, egg, brown sugar, and vanilla. In another bowl, stir together dry ingredients. Use a pastry blender or two knives to cut butter into dry ingredients until mixture resembles coarse meal. Stir in the currants and the milk mixture until mixture just forms a sticky dough. Drop by ⅓-cup measures into prepared muffin cups and bake in the middle of a preheated 400° oven for 15–18 minutes, or until golden.

"NOT REALLY FROM DEVONSHIRE" CREAM

It's almost impossible to find real English clotted cream here in the United States. This delicious dairy mixture makes an acceptable substitute. Real comfort food!

> ½ pint whipping cream
> 1 tablespoon sour cream
> 3 tablespoons confectioners' sugar

Chill bowl and beaters, then whip all ingredients together in a bowl. Keep refrigerated.

Something to Make
AN EASY, FLEECY TEA COZY

A tea cozy is really a warm little sweater or jacket for your teapot. It helps keep the tea warm while you linger over your cups of tea. Here's a very quick and very easy way to put together a tea cozy out of microfleece. It will look like a warm little ski hat with the handle and spout sticking out through little slits in the side—so they don't get too warm to handle.

To make it, you'll need about ½ yard of the fleece, plus standard sewing supplies—a tape measure, scissors, pins, sewing machine or needle and thread, and iron. In addition, you'll need a flat ruler, a pen or pencil, and a medium-sized rubber band.

To make the simplest kind of cozy, cut a rectangle of fleece in the following dimensions: (1) Height = height from table to top of teapot lid, measured with a tape measure loosely following the curves of the pot, plus 3¼ inches; (2) Width = the circumference of the pot at the widest point, not counting the handle and spout—you might have to estimate in some places—plus 1 inch.

Pin the short edges of the rectangle together with right sides facing and sew with a ½-inch seam. Press seam flat. Press under ½ inch along one long edge and stitch ¼ inch from fold to make a bottom hem. You should now have a tall fleece tube. Lay it flat with the

FUN FRIENDSHIP FACTS

Schoolgirls in the early nineteenth century often kept friendship albums that held poems and remembrances from their friends—loving inscriptions, locks of hair, paper cutouts, or bookmarks. The albums were treasured and often kept for years afterward, a handy place to store letters and to record births and deaths. The popularity of keeping friendship albums faded after the 1860s, when cameras became more widely available, but traces of this old practice can still be found in the custom of signing high school yearbooks: "When This You See, Remember Me."

seam right down the middle, but don't turn it right side out yet.

Set your teapot on a table or shelf where it is at your eye level. Stand the fleece tube next to it and mark a vertical slit on each side where the spout and handle should come out. With scissors, carefully cut these slits in each side.

To make the top fringe, use a pencil to draw a line around the top of the tube, about $2\frac{1}{2}$ inches from the edge. Make a series of cuts from the top edge down to this line. The cuts should be about $\frac{1}{2}$ inch apart but don't have to be exact—you can make them freehand. Now it is ready to be turned right side out.

Place the cozy over the top of the pot and pull the handle and spout through the side openings. With your hands, gather together the top edge above the lid and secure with a rubber band. Adjust the gathers as necessary. Then cover the rubber band with an 18-inch strip of fleece, preferably cut from the finished (selvage) edge of the fabric. Just tie it in a jaunty bow, and your warm, fuzzy tea cozy is ready to warm your teapot.

Something to Think About

THE ART OF FRIENDSHIP MAINTENANCE

It's one of the most important lessons we learn in life: We should always take care of the things we love. That's especially true of our treasured friendships. If we want them to last and grow, we need to invest some time and energy and thought into nurturing and maintaining them.

What is it—besides the occasional tea party—that keeps friendships alive and well? A lot of it just comes naturally. As we spend time together and enjoy each other's company and help each other, we're also taking care of our relationships. And yet a little deliberate nurturing goes a long way toward keeping a friendship in full bloom.

Most of the time, a little everyday tending is all that is needed—a phone call or e-mail, a touch or a hug, a thoughtful present, a silly surprise, or just a quiet cup of tea together. Such little gifts and gestures between friends keep us connected. Kept promises, too, help fertilize a friendship. So do the sacrifices we are willing to make for each other. And so does the willingness to address problems that arise between you, to talk the matter out or let it go and forgive.

Most of all, nurturing a friendship involves keeping each other in mind—even when we're not together. It means checking in on a regular basis, just to share our hearts and make sure that

TRADITIONAL ENGLISH TEA IS AN AFTERNOON AFFAIR, SERVED ANYTIME BETWEEN THREE AND SIX O'CLOCK—AND THE LATER IN THE DAY IT OCCURS, THE MORE HEARTY THE OFFERINGS. BUT THERE'S NO LAW THAT SAYS YOU CAN'T ENJOY A WARMING CUP WITH FRIENDS—AND A DELIGHTFUL TIME OF FELLOWSHIP—ANY TIME OF THE DAY, EVEN FOR BREAKFAST OR A NIGHTCAP.

everything is all right. It means seeking out ways to communicate, in ways little and large: "Oh yes, I'm still here. I know you're there, too. Never, ever forget that I care about you."

Here are just a few of the specific ways you can communicate just that to your most precious, most special friends and keep your friendships cozy and warm.

- *Make your friend's spiritual well-being a priority.* Pray for her always.
- *Give your friend her freedom.* Let her be who she is without trying to change her. Give her freedom to be different from you.
- *Give her the gift of your discretion.* Even with a close friend, some things may not need to be said. Others need to be said very carefully and gently.
- *Tell your friend what you like about her.* Offer verbal encouragement.
- *Make sure you have fun together.* If you have to, make dates to go out and play. And don't forget to enjoy a tea party now and then.
- *Say thank you again and again.* Make sure your friend knows how much you appreciate her.
- *Try to touch base even during busy times.* Even a one-minute phone call is enough to sing a song, read a short inspirational thought, or just say good morning.
- *Treasure your shared past.* Remind each other of your favorite memories.

*T*RUE FRIENDS...
accept each other
honor each other
care for each other
bear each other's burdens
encourage each other
open themselves to each other
forgive each other
build trust with each other
encourage each other's growth
give each other freedom
hold each other accountable
always, always love each other

March

A Heart-and-Hands Tea

She could not speak, but she did "hold on," and the warm grasp of the friendly human hand comforted her sore heart, and seemed to lead her nearer to the Divine arm which alone could uphold her in her trouble.

—Louisa May Alcott

It's wonderful to have friends when life is good, when we're happy and productive and confident. But it's when heartache strikes—when we face an illness or a loss or a disappointment—that we most deeply appreciate the bounty of true friendship. What an encouragement to have friends who will gather round in times of need, offering the gift of caring hearts and helping hands. And what a joy to be able to offer that gift of your heart and your hand to a hurting friend.

This teatime gathering is just one way you can offer the gift of loving support to a

friend who is struggling. It's an offering of heart and hope that will lift the spirits of all who attend and will send the guest of honor away with the fortifying knowledge that she is truly loved.

I'll never forget a luncheon I threw years ago for a friend who was fighting cancer and about to undergo a bone marrow transplant. A small group of us gathered with her in my home to show our support. After a simple meal in the dining room, we moved into another room, where I had set out crayons, markers, rubber stamps, and all manner of craft supplies. I handed our guest of honor a stack of heavy paper and instructed her to trace her hand onto each sheet—one sheet for each guest. The handprints were passed around the table, and each woman drew a freehand heart in the center of "her" handprint. Then we all had fun decorating our sheets with crayons and markers—it was a little like being back in kindergarten again.

But coloring was not really what this party was about. The real purpose was

SusanRios

our promise of ongoing love and prayer. For when we finished our handprints, we gathered together in a circle. Each of us put our hands on the hand of our sick friend and prayed for her. We hugged her and held her close. (We all cried together a little.) Then each of us took our decorated copy of her handprint home to post on our refrigerators—as a reminder to keep on praying.

What a poignant thing it was for me so many years later to be facing my own bone marrow transplant and to experience the same kind of loving support from my friends. During the months when I was waiting for the procedure, so many people held my hand over a cup of tea and prayed with me and hugged me. So many people symbolically placed their hands on mine as they placed my own handprint on their fridges.

I've come to believe that the loving support of people who care is one of the truest miracles we are given in our lifetimes. That means that when we use our caring and our imaginations to reach out to our friends, we are taking advantage of one of life's most precious opportunities—the

chance to be part of a miracle. That's exactly what can happen at a gathering such as a hearts-and-hands tea.

A Comforting Setting

For a dash of colorful cheer in a season when winter may be lingering, visit your grocery store or florist for pots of hopeful hyacinths in bright pink, lavender, and white. (Don't you just love their fragrance?) Cover the pots with swatches of print fabric in colors that coordinate with the blooms: just cut the fabric with pinking shears, fold up around the pots, secure with rubber bands, and hide the bands with cheery ribbon bows. Cluster them in the middle of a table draped with a solid pink or lavender cloth. Continue the theme around the house as well. Line up a few small pots on a windowsill, for instance, and be sure to place arrangements in other rooms the guests will visit. If you'd like to use the "heart-in-hand" activity described above, you can create a pretty but useful activity area by covering card tables with the same fabric you used to cover the pots.

Don't forget the bathroom when you're decorating your home for tea—it's the one place that almost everyone is bound to visit. Spiff up that room with fingertip towels that match your tea table and a few more pots of the hyacinths. For a subtle touch, create a simple graphic of a hand with a heart on it on a sheet of paper, color it, and slip it into an inexpensive frame to hang in the bathroom.

If you have china in pretty spring-hued florals, now is the time to use it. Simple white or clear glass will also serve, especially if you hem squares of the print fabric for generously sized napkins and fluff them into the teacups or pull them through heart-in-hand napkin rings (see directions on page 27).

$\mathscr{S}$OMETHING $\mathscr{D}$ELICIOUS

HEART-IN-HAND COOKIES

These are simple sugar cookies cut into the heart-and-hand shape and decorated beautifully. If you can't find a hand-shaped cookie cutter, you can trace a child's hand and make a cardboard template—or just cut small hearts out of large circles. This recipe will make about 3 dozen cookies, depending on the size of your cutters.

  2 cups butter, softened
  1 ½ cups sugar
  4 egg yolks
  2 teaspoons vanilla
  4 ½ cups unbleached flour
  ½ teaspoon salt
  1 tablespoon cinnamon
  1 hand-shaped cookie cutter about 3 inches
       long and at least 2 inches wide
  1 small heart-shaped cutter about 1 inch
       across
  red and blue food coloring

Preheat oven to 350°. Cream butter and sugar together in a mixer. Add egg yolks and vanilla. Mix well. Sift together flour, salt, and cinnamon. Beat into butter mixture. Chill dough about 1 hour. Roll out dough ¼ inch thick on lightly

floured board. Use the hand-shaped cutter to cut out hand-shaped cookies and the heart-shaped cutter to cut a small heart out of the center. Gather scraps (including cutout hearts) and reroll dough as needed. Place cookies on ungreased baking sheets and bake 12–14 minutes. Remove immediately and cool. Frost with thinned Royal Icing (recipe on page 9) tinted pink or lavender with food coloring.

GOLDEN CURRY CHICKEN SALAD SANDWICHES

The cashew nuts and raisins give these classic sandwiches a different twist. The recipe makes about 30 to 32 sandwiches.

2 cups very finely chopped chicken breast
½ cup each mayonnaise and sour cream
½ cup chopped celery
½ cup chopped cashew nuts
½ cup dried cherries or raisins
½ cup scallions, chopped, with plenty
    of green
2 teaspoons curry powder
nonstick cooking spray or a little canola oil
1 tablespoon lemon juice
salt and white pepper to taste
dash of bottled hot sauce (optional)
1 loaf of light wheat bread
unsalted butter, softened

In a bowl, mix chicken, celery, cashews, and scallions. Mix mayonnaise and sour cream in another bowl. Heat cooking spray or oil over medium heat in a nonstick skillet. Add curry powder and stir until blended. With a rubber scraper, scrape warmed curry powder into the mayonnaise–sour cream mixture. Add lemon and mix thoroughly. Stir this curry dressing into chicken mixture and mix well. Add salt, white pepper, and hot sauce to taste. To make sandwiches, spread slices of light wheat bread with unsalted butter. Spread filling between two slices of buttered bread (buttered side in). With a serrated knife, cut off crusts and then cut sandwiches into triangles to serve.

FUN FRIENDSHIP FACTS

Did you know that the Japanese word for friend is *tomadachi*? The Swahili word is *rafiki*. A warm-hearted Swedish friend is a *vän*. A German friend is a *Freund*—or *Freundin* if she's a woman—and Spanish women like to have fun with their *amigas*. If you're looking for Irish friends with a bit o' the Blarney, *cairdeas*, the Gaelic word for "friendship," is the word you need.

Something to Make
SALT DOUGH NAPKIN RINGS

As long you are making heart-in-hand cookies, you might also enjoy making some matching (inedible) ones to serve as napkin rings—they're sure to make guests smile, and they make a nice souvenir. These little ornaments are inexpensive and very easy to make out of salt dough, but plan to make them several days ahead of the party to allow plenty of drying time.

To make the dough, mix 2 cups of flour with 1 cup salt. Add water a little at a time (1/2 cup to 1 cup) until mixture forms a kneadable dough. Turn it out onto a lightly floured surface and knead dough for about ten minutes, then roll it out to about a 3/8-inch thickness. Cut out hand shapes with a cookie cutter or a cardboard template. Then use another cookie cutter to cut a heart shape from the center of each hand. Make the heart as large as you can, but leave at least half an inch of dough on either side of it. Place the cutouts on a cookie sheet and bake in a very slow oven (150° to 200°) until completely hard—at least several hours. You can also place them on a microwave-safe plate and bake them two at a time in the microwave for about 3–5 minutes, turning to cook evenly.

When the hardened napkin rings have cooled completely, paint them on both sides with acrylic paint in colors that match your place settings. (Leave a little brown edge showing so the napkin ring looks like an iced cookie.) You can add guests' names if you want and let the napkin rings serve as place cards. When paint is dry, coat front and back of napkin rings with several coats of polyurethane varnish. Let dry between coats.

To use, pull lightweight napkins through the heart-shaped hole in the center of the napkin rings. Place a "hand" atop each plate, propping it up on the thin edge and using the napkin to balance it.

Teatime Tidbits

WHEN TEA FIRST CAME TO ENGLAND, IT WAS CALLED BY ITS CANTONESE SLANG TERM—*CHA*. IT WAS ONLY AFTER THE BRITISH MOVED THEIR TEA TRADING BASE FROM CANTON TO AMOY THAT TEA BEGAN TO BE CALLED BY THE LOCAL WORD *T'E*—OR AS POPULARLY CALLED IN ENGLAND, *TAY* OR *TEE*.

Having a friend is one of the greatest gifts you've ever had. Cherish it and invest in it.

Something to Think About
THE ART OF HELPING A FRIEND IN NEED

Friends help friends—it's almost a definition of friendship. When any of us needs a loving heart or a helping hand, it's our friends we turn to, and the very acts of loving and helping in turn help cement our friendships. In fact, the relationships that last and grow over the years are often the ones that have been tested in the crucible of need. We all want to be that kind of friend to our chosen sisters, especially when they face hard times. Here are just a few specific ideas for how we can be a truly helpful friend in need:

- *Be there.* If you can, offer your physical presence and your practical help. Volunteer to answer the doorbell, make phone calls, do the laundry or grocery shopping, or sit by a bedside.
- *Pray for your friend on a regular basis.* Write it down on your to-do list. Don't underestimate the power of prayerful support.
- *Speak carefully.* It's easy to let thoughtless remarks slip out, and people in times of difficulty can be especially sensitive.
- *Listen, listen, listen.* Then listen some more…even when you've heard it all a million times. Don't put a timetable on your hurting friend's recovery.
- *Don't let your friend push you away.* If she lashes out in anger toward her situation, you may well become a target—just because you're there. Try to be extra tolerant and forgiving.
- *Be creative.* Carefully consider how you can

use your mind, your heart, your imagination, your gifts and talents most effectively to help your friend. Your bookkeeping skills may be more helpful than your cooking, your gardening expertise more appropriate than your organizational skills.

- *Let love be your motivator.* Consider the idea that love sometimes takes us places we thought we'd never go. Even people who "don't do hospitals" may find themselves by the bedside of those they truly care about.

- *Offer long-term support.* Even when a crisis is past, healing may take a while. Make a point of asking your friend from time to time how things are going and how she's feeling. Write little notes of support from time to time. Remind her of all she has to offer and that things will get better. Keep offering the gift of your hands and your heart.

- *Lean on a community of love.* Work together with other people who love your friend—her family,

other friends, her church. In this way you'll all support her better, and you'll support each other as well.

- *Remember to let your friend help you, too.* When you trust your friends with your needs and allow them to care for you, you are giving them a tangible gift of love. As your friend continues to heal from her time of need, consciously give her this gift by asking for her help and her prayers.

April

CELEBRATING FUN TOGETHER

A Shopping–Bag Tea

*Time spent in the company of a friend
is like a golden moment in our day.*
—Ron Lessin

What do you love to do best with your friends?

Some friends adore hiking together or playing tennis or riding horseback. Some enjoy sharing the experience of movies or theater or the opera or ballet. And almost everyone I know loves a day of shopping with friends—whether at the local mall, a posh antique store, a funky thrift shop, or even at the local Pic 'n' Save!

The point is not necessarily to buy—though I find it a joy to be with a friend who shares my particular power-shopping philosophy. The real fun of a day at the stores is exploring—enjoying all the beautiful colors and textures and smells, picking up interesting ideas, experiencing the thrill of nosing out a real bargain.

"Look at this!"

"Oh, this is great!"

"Hey, I'll bet I could make something like this myself."

And then, after a couple of hours on our feet, how wonderful it is to gather for tea in a sweet little corner shop or one of those elegant department-store tearooms, stashing your bags and parcels discreetly to the side, perching on dainty chairs, and eyeing with interest all the exquisite goodies in the display cases.

You can recreate that special sense of fashionable fun with a shopping-bag tea held in your very own home. It's a nice way to end an afternoon of fun with your friends—no matter what your particular fun has been. If you've actually been shopping, it's a lovely excuse to play show-and-tell with all your newfound treasures.

To maintain that air of elegant celebration, make this tea a dress-up affair. If you're gathering with just a few friends, put on your hats and

heels in the spirit of play—you could even get makeovers at the store before coming to tea. For a larger party, you could send written invitations and specify "church dress." In these days of dressing down for everything, the very act of looking spiffy will add a certain thrill to the activities.

An Elegant Setting

The key to capturing that tearoom elegance in your own home is to keep everything simple, clean, and lovely. For a fresh, up-to-date look, try a color scheme of white, clear glass, and greenery. Spread your table (or several small tables) with the crispest, snowiest linen you can find. Fill crystal clear vases with glass pebbles, then add interesting leaves and greenery in a variety of shapes and shades. You don't even need to add flowers, though a few stems of all-white blossoms can be quite effective. Try white tulips and long green leaves in tall glass vases, or group a cluster of small vases with simple leaves and lilies of the valley.

For place settings, choose your simplest, classiest, and most elegant china—or for a sleek look and very little cost, an inexpensive set of clear glass. Miniature gift bags at each place can lend a touch of whimsy; just fluff out a green linen napkin from the bag like tissue paper.

To continue the feel of a department-store tearoom, set out your assortment of tea foods on a sideboard in a splendid display. Guests can serve themselves buffet style, or you can arrange for "waiters" and "waitresses" (perhaps a couple of teenagers you've hired for the occasion) to take orders and serve. Deck a corner of the sideboard with a few more vases of greenery. (For an extra touch, stack a collection of real shopping bags and boxes from famous stores in several corners of the house.)

Make use of your most beautiful platters and bowls for the display of food, and if possible, place them at different levels. If you don't have cake and pie stands, you can make your own by carefully combining what you have. Glass circles stacked on custard cups, for instance, can make a beautiful tiered cookie stand. A simple platter perched atop a flat-bottomed bowl could serve as a dramatic cake stand—or stack two cake stands together for a high-rise display. Sturdy boxes covered with a cloth could serve as a multilevel base. Use your imagination, your sense of style, and your best engineering skills (stick the pieces together with floral clay, and don't use anything that's wobbly and might fall off!). Enjoy the fun and satisfaction that comes from creating something beautiful just for yourself and the friends of your heart.

$\mathcal{S}$OMETHING $\mathcal{D}$ELICIOUS

ANNE'S FAVORITE ICE CREAM WAFERS

Do you love mint chocolate chip ice cream? My friend Anne does, and she created these tender and elegant wafers just for this book. This recipe makes about 10 dozen small cookies.

> 1 cup butter, softened
> 1 cup granulated sugar, plus extra for
>   flattening cookies
> 1/2 teaspoon baking powder
> 1 egg
> 1 teaspoon vanilla
> 1/2 teaspoon peppermint extract
> 10 drops green food coloring
> 2 cups all-purpose flour
> 2/3 cup miniature chocolate chips
> nonstick cooking spray

In a large mixing bowl, beat butter with an electric mixer on medium to high speed for about 30 seconds. Add 1 cup sugar and baking powder and beat until fluffy. Beat in egg, extracts, and food coloring. In a separate bowl, combine flour and chocolate chips. With a wooden spoon, stir flour–chocolate chip mixture into butter mixture and mix until combined into a soft dough. Wrap dough in waxed paper and chill at least an hour.

When dough has chilled, unwrap it and cut into eight sections. Work with one section at a time, leaving the rest of the dough in the refrigerator. Place one section of the dough on a lightly floured surface and roll it into a log about 1 inch in diameter. The dough will be soft, so you might need to poke and pat a little as well as roll. With a sharp knife, cut the log into 1/2-inch slices. Quickly roll the slices into balls about 3/4 of an inch in diameter. Place about 2 inches apart on an ungreased cookie sheet and flatten each ball to 1/4-inch thickness with the bottom of a glass sprayed with cooking spray and dipped in additional sugar.

Bake cookies at 375° for 6–8 minutes or until edges are set but not brown. Transfer to a wire rack to cool.

ELEGANT FRUIT TARTLETS

These elegant little tarts are made with a shortbread cookie crust that requires no rolling. Make them with a variety of colorful fruits—or concentrate on just one that is in season.

1 stick butter, softened

1/3 cup sugar

1 1/4 cups all-purpose flour

1 cup seedless raspberry jam

1 jar homemade or commercial lemon curd

1 pint fresh fruit—blueberries, raspberries, strawberries, kiwi, peaches

lemon juice if needed to keep fruit from turning brown

Preheat oven to 350°. Butter miniature muffin pans well or spray with nonstick cooking spray. Cream together butter and sugar until light and fluffy. Add flour and blend until just combined. Then press rounded teaspoons of dough evenly into bottom and up sides of miniature muffin cups. (I found it easier to roll the dough into balls, press them down evenly into the cups, then use my finger and a cork to work the dough into a tart-shell shape.) Chill these shells 15 minutes, then bake in middle of preheated oven for 10-15 minutes or until golden around edges. Let cool 5 minutes, then loosen shells with tip of a sharp knife, transfer to racks, and let cool completely. You can make these shells a few days ahead of time and store them in a covered container.

When ready to serve, spread a small amount of raspberry jelly in the bottom of each shell, add a small dollop of lemon curd, then top with a few pieces of fresh fruit—2 or 3 blueberries, a single raspberry, a wedge of kiwi, or a piece of strawberry. (If the fruit browns easily, toss in lemon juice first.) For a delicious variation on this recipe, omit the jam and lemon curd. Arrange the fruit on the tart shells and coat with a glaze of melted apple jelly.

Teatime Tidbits

THE TERM "ORANGE PEKOE TEA" REFERS TO THE DUTCH HOUSE OF ORANGE AND TRADITIONALLY LABELS HIGH-QUALITY TEA MADE FROM THE WHOLE LEAF. IT HAS NOTHING WHATSOEVER TO DO WITH CITRUS FRUIT!

Something to Make
ELEGANT ETCHING

You can make your inexpensive glass tea dishes even more elegant by etching them with a delicate design—flowers, ivy leaves, or just a simple border. Glass etching takes a little bit of care because you'll be working with an acid, but it's not difficult or time consuming. Try it out by decorating a single plate or platter—you might eventually graduate to an entire tea set.

To make your etched glass creation, you'll need a piece of glass to etch (I recommend starting with something simple and relatively flat, like a plate), commercial etching cream from a craft store, a commercial glass-etching stencil, and an inexpensive paintbrush or wooden craft stick. You'll also need commercial glass cleaner for cleaning the glass and some rubber gloves and goggles to protect you from any accidental splashes.

Clean your glass item thoroughly with glass cleaner before you start and wipe it dry with a clean, lint-free cloth. Next, you'll need to prepare the stencil. Commercially made stencils come with their own instructions for sticking the stencil to the glass. Follow those directions carefully.

Now put on your gloves and goggles! Following the directions on the bottle of etching cream, use a wooden craft stick or an old paintbrush to apply etching cream. Apply thickly—you shouldn't be able to see the design through the cream—and allow to sit for the amount of time indicated on the bottle—anywhere from one to ten minutes. Then, still wearing gloves and goggles, rinse the etching cream off under clear running water. Be sure to rinse completely and keep the cream off any areas you don't want etched. Pay special attention to the edges of your design because the cream can accumulate there.

When the glass item (and the brush) is cleaned off, remove the stencil. (Stubborn pieces will come off with glass cleaner and a plastic "scrubbie.") Dry off the glass with a towel—and admire your beautiful design.

One of the things I like about our friendship is that I know you think I'm a good friend.

34

Something to Think About
IDEAS FOR FUN AFTERNOONS TOGETHER

What's the point of having a friend if you don't do things together? Here's a whole list of ideas for fun your friends can share before, after, or even during a wonderful shopping-bag tea! Use it to spark your own ideas of something new you can do together.

- *Read a book* or play aloud or discuss an article you've all read.
- *Pack a lunch* in backpacks and take a long walk.
- *Make a group appointment at a day spa*—or get together to give your own facials, massages, or whatever.
- *Spend an Indian summer afternoon planting bulbs* in all your yards.
- *Hold a six-week group Bible study* just for your group of friends.
- *Drive to a nearby small town* and have lunch in a little place you've never been before.
- *Rent a movie* and gather all your families together to watch it on a big screen.
- *Play music together* or sing.
- *Schedule a "Put in Album" day* for all those photos that have piled up.
- *On another day, spend the afternoon thumbing through albums* and looking at photos of each other from grade school, high school, and college.
- *Spend your lunch hour at the skating rink.*
- *Make a date to attend the matinee of the newest "chick flick" in town.* Bring lots of tissues.
- *Have breakfast together very early on a Friday or Saturday and then go garage-sale hopping.* Bring a newspaper, a local map, and some cash—many sales don't take checks.
- *Play a game* of Monopoly, Scrabble, or chess.

May
CELEBRATING MILESTONES
A "Good for You!" Tea

When we reach out to others, they reach out to us. It's a two-way street, a street practically lined with balloons and streamers in celebration of the unique bonds of friendship.

—Luci Swindoll

"Hooray for you!"

"Good work!"

"I'm so happy you're happy!"

Who doesn't love to hear those kinds of words? There's so much we can accomplish in life if we know someone is cheering us on. And that's part of what friends are for. Applauding each other's accomplishments and recognizing each other's milestones is simply something that friends *do*. We need our friends to help us celebrate just as surely as we need friends to help us navigate hard times.

Think back on the important occasions of your life—landmark birthdays, religious ceremonies, graduations, your wedding, the arrival of your children. Can you remember those days without also remembering the faces of special friends who shared them with you? I can't!

And don't you feel an important bond with those friends who allowed you to share their own times of joy and celebration? That's especially true for me. My memories of my friends are inescapably tied in with my memories of shared birthdays and anniversaries and weddings and other celebrations.

All this is good reason to strengthen your connection with current friends by gathering together to celebrate the good things that happen in your lives.

Has one of your friends landed a new job, earned a diploma, or acquired a new grandbaby? Is someone you care about approaching a special anniversary? Has something wonderful happened—like a new house or

twenty-pound weight loss—that calls for shared rejoicing? You can beautifully celebrate both the occasion and your wonderful friendships by inviting a group of friends to a "good for you!" tea. It's a warm, colorful hurrah that can't help but draw you all closer together.

A tea of this sort adapts beautifully for traditional celebrations—it'll give a different twist to wedding or baby showers, a birthday, or a commemorative holiday such as Mother's Day. And keep in mind that the "good for you" doesn't have to be just for one person! This special teatime can easily become a "good for us" party that celebrates a group accomplishment—or even just your friendship itself.

When you invite guests to the tea, make sure you inform them of the party's purpose—and whether gifts would be expected. Then, after the party starts, plan on a little bit of pomp and ceremony. Consider a little testimonial, a speech from the guest of honor, a toast with teacups. The point is to do whatever you can think of to make a "big deal" out of the celebration, to make it feel memorable to the one you are celebrating. Honor her with a corsage in colors to match your tea. Present her with gifts, if appropriate, or, for a touch of whimsy, a laurel wreath or "Queen for a Day" crown.

Be sure and take lots of photographs of the occasion and plan to put them in an album or scrapbook for the honoree. And don't forget to gather everyone for a group shot—a beautiful visual record of friends who care enough to celebrate together.

A Festive Setting

The scene for *any* celebration should be festive and colorful.

The scene for a teatime celebration should be festive, colorful, and *beautiful*.

You can do this easily by thinking: *confetti with class*. Decorate in an array of confetti colors, even with balloons and streamers, but use your most beautiful linens and china as well. Keep the mood festive and even whimsical, but with a slightly formal, "dress up" feel to it.

Choose your confetti color scheme according to the colors of your dishes or your room. If you have a lovely pink-sprigged teapot, pick confetti colors in pastels of pink, spring green, yellow, and blue. If you love your cobalt-and-white cups and saucers, you might choose primary colors with blue predominating. If you use simple white china or clear glass, of course, you can pick your favorites.

A simple white cloth can serve as a background on your tea table. Sprinkle it with confetti you've purchased from a party shop or made yourself. (Party shops usually stock supplies of ready-made confetti, or you can cut your own from colored paper using scissors or a hole punch.) Just make sure the pieces are small enough and soft

Teatime Tidbits

RECENT STUDIES INDICATE THAT TEA IN GENERAL—AND GREEN TEA IN PARTICULAR—CAN BE NOT ONLY GOOD, BUT GOOD FOR YOU. POWERFUL ANTIOXIDANTS IN THE TEA LEAVES HELP PREVENT FREE-RADICAL DAMAGE TO CELLS AND MAY HELP PREVENT MALIGNANCIES. THEY MAY ALSO HELP LOWER CHOLESTEROL, FIGHT BACTERIA AND VIRUSES, AND EVEN HELP THE BODY BURN CALORIES FASTER!

FUN FRIENDSHIP FACTS

Romantic love has probably been the number-one song topic through the ages, but some great songs have also been written about friendship and sung to friends. Here are some highlights from the past few centuries!

- John Fawcett, "Blessed Be the Tie That Binds" (1782)
- Robert Burns, "Auld Lang Syne" (1798)
- Harry Woods, "Side by Side" (1927)
- Cole Porter, "Friendship" (1939)
- Saxie Dowell, "Oh Playmate, Come Out and Play with Me" (1940)
- Richard Rodgers and Oscar Hammerstein, "Getting to Know You" (1951)
- Ben E. King, Jerry Leiber, and Mike Stoller, "Stand by Me" (1961)
- John Lennon and Paul McCartney, "In My Life" (1965)
- Carole King, "You've Got a Friend" (1971)
- Andrew Gold, "Thank You for Being a Friend" (1978)
- Carol Bayer Sager and Burt Bacharach, "That's What Friends Are For" (1982)
- Michael W. Smith and Deborah Smith, "Friends" (1982)
- Point of Grace, "Circle of Friends" (1996)

enough to be vacuumed easily later! If you can find them, a beautiful alternative to paper confetti would be multicolored flower petals. Sometimes you can order these by mail (try an Internet search!)—or a florist may be willing to give you petals from shattered blossoms. If you have a garden, of course, you can gather your own.

Instead of napkins that match the tablecloth, an array of different-colored cloth napkins will add to the sense of festivity. Try fluffing them out like flowers in a pretty basket or a wide-mouthed vase or from individual teacups. Another fun possibility would be to use fabric markers to sprinkle a confetti border on a set of white cotton napkins and pull each through a colorful napkin ring.

For a centerpiece, choose a low dish and arrange an assortment of flowers in colors that match your confetti colors. (If you're unsure of your skills in this area, ask a florist to do this for you.) A few miniature Mylar balloons attached to florists' spikes add an extra festive touch. For a whimsical touch, tuck one end of colorful ribbons into the arrangement and let their loose ends trail out onto the table like streamers.

$\mathscr{S}$OMETHING $\mathscr{D}$ELICIOUS

CELEBRATION SANDWICHES

These colorful sandwiches will really tingle your taste-buds and delight your eye.

> 2 6-ounce cans water-packed flake tuna, drained
> 2 tablespoons mayonnaise
> 4 teaspoons finely diced green bell pepper
> 4 teaspoons finely diced red bell pepper
> 2 tablespoons red onion, finely diced
> ½ teaspoon chopped fresh parsley
> 1 teaspoon rice wine vinegar
> ½ teaspoon lemon juice
> 7 drops hot pepper sauce
> salt and white pepper to taste
> 1 loaf fine-textured white or wheat bread
> unsalted butter, softened

Combine all ingredients but bread and butter and mix well. Refrigerate at least one hour. Spread each slice of bread with softened butter. Spread half the slices with tuna mixture, then top with remaining slices. With a serrated knife, cut off

crusts and cut sandwiches into three or four fingers. Wrap tightly in plastic wrap or cover with a damp tea towel until ready to serve.

"EASY AS CAKE" CONFETTI COOKIES

These colorful cookies look very cheerful when arranged on a glass plate with a colored doily. If you prefer, you can add nuts instead of the chocolate chips—or omit the coconut and chips entirely. This recipe makes 4 to 5 dozen cookies.

> nonstick cooking spray
> 1 8-ounce package cream cheese, room temperature
> 2 eggs
> 1 box confetti cake mix
> ½ cup coconut
> ½ cup white chocolate chips

Preheat oven to 350°. Lightly grease cookie sheets with cooking spray. In a bowl, beat cream cheese and egg together with an electric mixer. Add cake mix, coconut, and white chocolate chips and mix well. Drop by teaspoonfuls onto cookie sheet. (Dough will be sticky. If you wish, you can chill for several hours to make it easier to handle.) With wet fingers, press down cookies a little and smooth edges. Bake cookies at 350° for 8–10 minutes, until edges brown. Allow to cool 1 minute on cookie sheet, then remove to wire racks to cool completely.

Something to Make
A CELEBRATION TABLE

If you own a glass-topped dining table, you can add a refreshing twist to your celebration table with just a little paint. Simply clean the underside of your table with commercial glass cleaner and use acrylic craft paints to dot colorful confetti directly on the glass.

If you like, you could even get very creative and paint festive garlands around the table's edge or words of congratulations to the guest of honor—just remember to paint backward so the words will read correctly from the top. This technique adapts very easily to any kind of glass—from the inside of the storm door to the coffee tables in the living room or even your glass plates. (Just be sure to paint on the undersides so that the paint doesn't interfere with the food.) When you're through with the party, you'll find the paint comes off easily with a spritz of glass cleaner and some clean paper towels.

Something to Think About
OCCASIONS TO CELEBRATE

"You're a very festive person."

I once heard one friend say that about another, and I think it was one of the nicest compliments I've ever heard. In fact, one of my goals in life is to learn to be an even more festive person. I want to be someone who really notices the beautiful things God has put in my life. I want to celebrate the gift of my own days and the gift of the people I've been given to love. I want to mark the passages of the seasons, both in the year and in my lifetime—to learn the art of true thankfulness, to "rejoice in the Lord always" and celebrate His goodness with the ones I love.

Don't you want to be a festive person, too? Whether you are a "party type" or prefer quieter ceremonies of rejoicing, you nurture your relationships and strengthen the bonds of friendship whenever you stage a teatime celebration. Here are just a few of the possible occasions you can celebrate with your friends and a cup of tea:

- *Mother's Day*—a celebration tea for your friends and their mothers.
- *Graduation*—for young friends and for hard-working friends who have gone back to school.
- *A birthday*—of course, with special attention to those "big 0" birthdays such as twenty, thirty, forty, and beyond!
- *The anniversary of a time your group of friends first met.* (First day of college? First day of kindergarten for your kids?)
- *A new job, new business, or really important contract.*
- *The completion of an athletic event*—a 5K race or a marathon.
- *The receipt of good news.*
- *A pregnancy or adoption*—or the baptism or dedication of an infant.
- *An engagement.*
- *A new house*—or finally selling one!
- *A good day.*
- *The end of a really bad day*!

The friendships we treasure most dearly are the ones in which we feel, "Wow, how did I deserve this?"

43

June
CELEBRATING TOGETHERNESS

A "Tea Potluck" for Your Larger Circle of Friends

Our friends are the continuous threads that help hold our lives together.
—Sarah Ban Breathnach

Warm, wonderful, intimate teas don't have to be just for two or three—or even six or seven—special friends. With a little planning and care, you can extend that delicious sense of closeness and empathy to a much larger group—your office, the women in your church, a club meeting, a conference, or some other event.

Hosting such a tea could even be a fun project for your smaller group of friends. You could get together and plan an elegant tea for your larger circle of acquaintances.

And here's a fun idea: Why not lighten the load a little by holding a tea "potluck"? It's not strictly traditional, but it can easily fit the warm, embracing spirit of the tea party—plus it's a great way to widen your circle of friends, expand your recipe files, and enjoy a wonderful time.

Here's how it works. You and your planning partners do the planning and invite the guests. You provide the beautiful room, the program, and, of course, the tea. But you invite each guest to bring a delectable teatime treat to share. If you ask them to bring the recipes as well, you can compile them into a booklet later and make them available to everyone who attended.

For a large group, it usually works best to assign each guest to a specific table—use place cards to make the places. Each table should have a hostess whose responsibility is to decorate the table, serve the tea, and make sure each guest is happy.

As with any potluck, part of the fun of this party will be simply sampling the goodies and enjoying the fellowship, but some form of entertainment would add to the fun. Choose entertainment appropriate to the teatime setting and to your particular gathering. A string quartet, a pianist, a harpist, or a cellist would be lovely, but an inspirational talk or a dramatic reading might also serve. You don't necessarily have to spend a lot of money for someone to perform. A musical group from a local high school or college or a local amateur ensemble might be happy to play for little or nothing. Or members of your group might like to showcase their talents—an afternoon's entertainment in the classic Victorian sense.

A Beautiful Setting

The trick to hosting a successful tea for a large group is to handle the logistics of serving more people while maintaining the teatime sense of intimacy. Probably the best way to do this is to use round tables that seat no more than six or eight. Since variety is the heart of a potluck, why not decorate the tables individually as well—perhaps even assigning a different person to decorate each table? Provide a sense of unity by draping the tables in identical solid-colored cloths from a rental agency—a deep blue or green would serve this purpose beautifully, although white is always appropriate as well. Then ask each hostess to use her imagination in providing the little extras that make a table lovely—lace tea cloths to top the table, placemats or place cards for individual settings, solid or floral napkins, and decorations such as a centerpiece or napkin rings. Hostesses could even hang swags of tulle or ivy around the sides of the table or sew dainty slipcovers for the backs of chairs. (I've found that pillowcases can make wonderful coverings for metal folding chairs. They are inexpensive and can be decorated any way you like.)

If you wish, you can designate a common theme to unify all the diverse settings and give your hostesses a place to begin. Since roses are the designated flower for June, all the tables could be decorated around a rose theme. Another lovely idea would be to decorate with candles and oil lamps, with extra teapots that serve as vases, or with trailing ivy—long a beautiful symbol of friendship.

For the actual table settings, you have several choices. The individuals decorating the tables might enjoy using their own sets, borrowing a variety from friends, or even calling for "potluck" from those assigned to their tables. (Remember that mismatched table settings can be charming.) For large groups, however, it might make sense to rent simple white or gold-banded plates or to use the dishes that come with the facility where the tea is to be held. (Many churches, for instance, have a large collection.) The table linens and centerpieces will still provide plenty of variety.

Although the nature of a potluck dictates that guests will need to serve themselves from a buffet table, plan to serve the tea itself at the table. Ideally, the hostess of each table would serve from a tea service placed on a tea cart beside her table, but this would depend on how many tea services and carts are available. Alternately, you could have a large tea service or samovar available at your buffet table—but make sure that someone is still available to serve every cup individually.

Make the serving table itself a work of art even before the potluck offerings arrive. A long buffet table usually works best for this purpose. Drape it with undercloths to match the other tables and a lovely topping—a series of square lace cloths placed diagonally will top a lengthy table beautifully. Add a narrow centerpiece to match your theme, and scatter the rest of the table with snippets of matching flowers or greenery—rosebuds or trailing ivy among the plates of goodies. If you are planning to serve the tea from the buffet table, place the tea service at one end. If you wish, you could serve either coffee or an iced-tea punch from the other end.

Something Delicious

TEA CONCENTRATE FOR A CROWD

You can brew this concentrate up to two hours ahead and still serve hot, perfectly brewed tea to your guests. This recipe makes about fifty cups of tea, but you can make more or less concentrate according to your needs. Just remember: To make tea in quantity, don't brew longer—use more tea!

1½ cups loose tea or 16 family-size tea bags
2½ quarts boiling water

Pour boiling water over tea in a large nonmetallic container such as an earthenware crock. Let steep for five minutes, then strain the tea leaves or remove the tea bags. Store concentrate at room temperature until needed. To serve, use about two tablespoons of concentrate per five-ounce cup—or about three parts of water to every part concentrate. Simply place the desired amount of the concentrate in a cup or pot and then add the hot water.

Note: This concentrate also makes delicious iced tea. Put four tablespoons in an eight-ounce glass of water, then add water and ice.

ORANGE ALMOND STICKY ROLLS

These are the very definition of easy and delicious!

1 8-ounce package refrigerated crescent
  dinner rolls
1 tablespoon melted butter
⅓ cup brown sugar
¼ teaspoon ground cinnamon
1 tablespoon grated orange peel
¼ cup finely slivered almonds, plus more to
  sprinkle
⅔ cup sifted confectioners' sugar
2 tablespoons frozen orange juice-
  concentrate
2 teaspoons water
⅛ teaspoon almond extract

Heat oven to 375°. Lightly grease a miniature muffin pan. On a lightly floured surface, unroll the crescent-roll dough and press the perforations to seal the dough into one large rectangle. Brush this dough rectangle with melted butter. In a small bowl, combine sugar, cinnamon, orange peel, and ¼ cup finely slivered almonds and

Teatime Tidbits

TEATIME CAN BE AS SIMPLE AS A BREWED CUP AND A COOKIE, BUT A CERTAIN ARRAY OF FOODS HAS BECOME TRADITIONAL FOR MORE FORMAL TEAS. A TYPICAL TEA TABLE MIGHT HOLD SAVORY TIDBITS SUCH AS SPICED NUTS OR CHEESE PUFFS, DAINTY SANDWICHES, BUTTERY SCONES, AND FRESH FRUIT AS WELL AS A VARIETY OF SWEET GOODIES SUCH AS COOKIES, TARTS, PETITS FOURS, AND CAKES.

sprinkle evenly over the dough. Starting at one long side, roll up the dough jellyroll fashion. Place on a cutting board with seam down and cut into 1-inch slices. Place each slice with cut side down into a lightly greased miniature muffin pan. Bake at 375° for 11–13 minutes or until golden. While rolls are baking, combine powdered sugar and orange-juice concentrate. Add water and extract and stir until smooth. When rolls are done, remove them from the pans immediately and drizzle them with orange glaze. Sprinkle with more slivered almonds.

Something to Make
TEAPOT PLACE CARDS

Use the same salt dough recipe you used in the Heart-and-Hands Tea (p. 27) to make beautiful place cards for your tea tables. Simply mix and roll the dough, then use cookie cutters to cut into desired shapes—a teapot would be especially cute. In addition, for each two place cards, cut a 2-by-4-inch rectangle out of the rolled dough. Cut the rectangle from corner to corner to make two long triangles. These will be the props that hold the place cards upright. Bake the props along with the place cards. When the dough has cooled, paint the place cards with acrylic paint and then paint the guest's name on top. Let paint dry, then spray front and back with several layers of polyurethane varnish. Spray the triangular cutouts as well. When all is dry, use a hot-glue gun to attach the two-inch edge of the triangle to the bottom of the place cards.

Note: if you want the place cards to lean back slightly, experiment with the shape of the

FUN FRIENDSHIP FACTS

In 1926, as a token of international friendship, 12,789 dolls were collected from American children and sent to Japan for the *Hina Matsuri,* or Doll Festival. In return, Japanese artists were commissioned to create 58 beautifully dressed *Torei Ningyo* (ambassador dolls) to send to the U.S. During World War II, many of these friendship dolls were destroyed in both countries, but others were hidden away and protected. Today, hundreds of the American dolls have been found in Japan, and more than 44 of the Japanese dolls survive in America. Now, American and Japanese children have begun sending dolls back and forth again as a token of friendship, proving once again what a Japanese newspaper reported in 1927: "The exchange of dolls is the exchange of hearts."

bread dough prop. If you trim the 2-inch edge at a little more of an angle, the place card will lean back just a little bit, showing off the name and graciously inviting your friends to sit down and take tea.

Something to Think About
CIRCLES OF FRIENDSHIP

Our friendships aren't all the same—and I think that's a very good thing. Though our closest friendships are a beautiful gift, our hearts weren't made to sustain more than a few of these at a time. There aren't enough moments in our lives to nurture a large number of intimate, intense relationships. But thank God for the joy of the various kinds of friendships that surround our lives like rippling rings on a pond!

Some of our friends, for instance, are *everyday* friends—the neighbors and colleagues we see on a daily basis. We do favors for each other, borrow cups of sugar, swap stories over the back fence or at the water cooler. We are a pleasant part of the fabric of each other's lives—and in a crisis, we are always ready to step in and help.

And then there are the friends who share a more specialized aspect of our lives. We may know each other at church or a club meeting. We may share an interest in books or animals or help each other in a support group that addresses a shared problem. Though we may see these people only once a week, or once a month, still they play an important role in our lives.

Common memories bind us together with some friends. We went to school together, or we played together as children, or our own children were small together—and so they became a part of our lives. Some of these people we may still see often; others become Christmas-card friends. A special few may become touchstones with whom we periodically reunite—friends who keep us grounded by reminding us who we've been and how we've changed. Others drop out of sight, surfacing occasionally in our thoughts and receiving the benediction of our good wishes.

Not all of our friendships are destined to last. Some grow out of the intensity of a shared project or experience—working together on a committee, training for a race, supporting each other in the dismal intimacy of a hospital waiting room. These relationships may influence us enormously, imprinting our memories with friendship—yet fade away when the project is finished or the crisis is over.

All of these circles of our friendships enrich our lives. In a sense, they make us who we are, and they are all important. But most important of all are the special friends, the forever friends, the friends of the heart. These are the unforgettable people who, for whatever reason, stake a permanent claim in our very souls. These are our chosen sisters, the ones who leave us pondering what we ever did to deserve them—and best of all, they feel the same way about us.

Amid all the circles of our friendships, they are the ones who live at the living center of our lives.

No matter how many friends you have, you have them one at a time.

July
CELEBRATING NATURE

Tea by the Sea—or Anywhere!

My soul is full of longing
For the secret of the sea,
And the heart of the great ocean
Sends a thrilling pulse through me.

—Henry Wadsworth Longfellow

Tea parties don't all have to be carefully planned indoor affairs. Some of my most enjoyable times have been those when a friend and I put together some quick goodies, packed up a basket, and headed for a favorite spot, indoors or out. Almost any beautiful day is a perfect excuse for a spontaneous picnic tea party. Almost any setting will serve, though my favorite has always been the beach—a summer-day staple in Southern California, where I grew up.

What if the day is rainy or you live far from the shore? You can re-create that sunny beach feeling on your deck, at a lakeside cabin, or even in your cheerfully decorated dining room. Just hang some wind chimes, put Hawaiian music on a CD player, set out some luscious summery tea food, and invite good friends who love the sand and sea as much as you do.

This is one tea party that can work equally well for two people or a dozen. Try to keep the setting simple and spontaneous. Ask your guests to dress up in filmy romantic dresses and hats or flowing Hawaiian brights. (You provide the leis!) Refine the usual beach casualness with the elegance of teatime manners—and enjoy that special feeling that comes with dressing up and sipping tea…even by the beautiful sea.

You don't really need a program or entertainment for an outdoor tea. Just enjoying the outdoors together with good friends is entertainment enough. A walk together along a pier or down by the sand or just through the park would be a perfect way to enjoy

tea together, either working up an appetite or working off the delicious teatime calories!

And remember that you can transfer that special outdoor-tea feeling to settings other than the beach. Use your imagination to plan a woodland tea (with ferns and mosses), an autumn tea (with acorns and wonderful colored leaves), a backyard tea (with gingham and daisies on a picnic table), or—most traditional of all—a beautiful garden tea. Whether your tea is simple and spontaneous or carefully planned, the point of "tea by the sea" or anywhere outdoors is to enjoy your friends and to celebrate the gifts of God's creation together.

A Breezy Setting

If you're enjoying tea by the sea for two, you'll want to keep the decorations very simple—perhaps just a coconut-scented candle and some shells in addition to your tea service. Just arrange all your goodies on a single serving plate and kick back in lounge chairs with the tea between you. A larger party will be a little more elaborate, but it can still have that easygoing, spontaneous air. A mix of beachtime casual and teatime formal can be especially charming—with the rough textures of sand playing up the smoothness of good linen and delicate china.

If you can locate a fine-textured fishnet, drape it over your white or seaside pastel tablecloth for an eye-catching contrast. Then place a mirror tile or circle of glass in the center of the table to hold an arrangement of sand (from a garden or home center), shells and driftwood (from the beach or a hobby shop), and candles. Simple glass votives anchored in the sand will work nicely—or you can half fill a glass "chimney" with sand and shells that anchor a large pillar candle. Use your imagination to fill out the arrangement with aquatic extras—a model lighthouse or boat, some colorful carved fish from an import shop, bits of polished beach glass—or go for a South Seas flavor with colorful potted orchids or hibiscus. (Be sure to tuck a big blossom behind your ear.)

Choose napkins in an array of beach colors—sandy pinks, peaches, greens, blues, and beige—or lively Hawaiian-shirt prints and hot-glue pieces of shell or driftwood to purchased napkin rings to hold them in place. Look for ways you can continue the beach theme throughout the house as well.

You could festoon the front lawn with tiki lanterns, hot-glue shells to a grapevine wreath for the door, dress a small table in a grass skirt (just pin it to the tablecloth), perch a papier-mâché parrot in a corner, or strategically place a pair of thongs and a colorful beach towel outside the shower. After that, all you have to do is put on a CD of sea sounds, Beach Boys, or Hawaiian guitar, put on your summer straw hat and sandals, and invite your guests to relax.

Can't you just smell that salt air—mingling with the luscious aromas of coconut, pineapple, and fruit-flavored tea?

Something Delicious

TROPICAL TEA

Tea doesn't have to be hot, even for a tea party. On steamy summertime days, nothing is more refreshing than a big glass of iced tea—or a fruity tea punch like this one, served in frosted glasses with a skewer of tropical fruit or a little umbrella. This recipe makes about 15 8-ounce glasses or 30 punch cups.

1 cup water
1 ¼ cups sugar
3 cups freshly brewed strong tea
3 cups orange juice
1 cup lemon juice

2 cups pineapple juice
1 quart club soda or seltzer
ice cubes, preferably made from orange or
  pineapple juice

Boil the water and sugar together for five minutes to make a syrup. Mix the tea and juices together, then stir in the sugar syrup. Cover and chill overnight. When ready to serve, fill glass or cup half full with concentrate, add ice, then top off glass with seltzer or club soda. If you prefer, place the entire recipe in a punch bowl, float an ice ring made from juices, and serve.

COCONUT DREAM POUND CAKE

Close your eyes and imagine yourself taking tea on a South Seas island as you enjoy this coconut pound cake. This recipe makes one 9-inch loaf and will serve at least twelve. Slice it thinly—it's very rich!

- 3/4 cup butter
- 1 1/2 cups sugar
- 3 eggs
- 1 1/2 cups flour
- 1/4 teaspoon soda
- 1/4 teaspoon salt
- 1/4 cup sour cream
- 1/2 cup sweetened flake coconut, plus extra for topping
- 1/2 cup chopped unsalted macadamia nuts
- 1/2 teaspoon coconut flavoring, plus 1/2 teaspoon for topping
- 2/3 cup confectioners' sugar
- 2 tablespoons water

Preheat oven to 325°; grease and flour a 9-inch loaf pan. Cream butter and sugar together, then add eggs one at a time, beating well after each addition. In separate bowl, sift flour, soda, and salt together. Add to butter mixture alternately with sour cream. Blend in 1/2 cup coconut, the nuts, and 1/2 teaspoon coconut flavoring. Pour batter into loaf pan, smooth top, and bake 60–80 minutes or until skewer inserted in middle comes out clean. Cool at least twenty minutes in pan, then remove to wire rack and cool completely. Mix the confectioners sugar with 1/2 teaspoon coconut flavoring and 2 tablespoons water. Mix to form glaze and spread on top of cake. Sprinkle with more coconut.

Note: If you cannot find unsalted macadamia nuts, buy the salted kind and rinse them before using. Reduce the amount of salt in recipe.

Something to Make
"By the Sea" Napkins

It's easy and fun to make your own beach-themed napkins using fabric-transfer paper for either a color laser copier or your ink-jet printer. Both kinds of paper are available at office supply stores or craft stores, and many copy centers will either supply the paper or run your paper through their copiers. (The transfers made with color copiers tend to be of better quality than the ink-jet printer ones, although they are not as convenient.)

To make a set of napkins using a color copier, either purchase or make solid-color napkins in a smooth, medium-weight cotton or cotton blend. (A single sheet from a discount or closeout store will make an entire set—just turn under the edges and hem.)

The design for your napkins could be a shell, sea horse, abstract waves, or any other "seaside" motif in a color that matches the napkins. You can draw it freehand with markers or crayons, stamp it with a rubber stamp inked in various colors with a marking pen, or print out a clip art design from your computer. Use a larger motif for the corners of the napkins, a smaller design to be printed as a border around the edges, or both.

Once you have a design or designs that you like, use a color copier to

FUN FRIENDSHIP FACTS

Studies show that men and women differ in what they usually expect from their friendships. While men's friendships tend to be more centered about companionship and particular activities—"fishing buddies," "workout partners," and so on—women's friendships usually focus more on closeness and emotional attachment—sharing feelings, thoughts, experiences, and support.

copy paper, have it copied onto the special transfer paper. Then all you have to do is cut the designs apart, position them on the napkins, and heat-set them with an iron. Follow the directions on the package of transfer paper carefully for this. Once the design is set, it will be washable and wonderful—perfect for "tea by the sea" whenever you desire.

Something to Think About
COMING OUT TO PLAY

"Can you come out and play?"

Remember when those were the words you wanted most to hear?

When we were little, in fact, playing was the whole point of having friends. Our play was really our work, of course; it was the way we learned. But oh, how we loved to do it together—riding bikes, jumping rope, building sand castles at the beach, playing house, and finding won-derful hidey holes in the trees and bushes of our backyards.

make several copies. Cut them out, arrange them together on a sheet of paper, and copy again until you have a full sheet of paper covered with designs. Keep in mind that they will be reversed on the final napkin. Remember, too, that each individual design will become a nonreusable iron-on transfer, so you need a full set for each napkin—plus a few extra for practice in applying the designs. You'll save money by arranging as many designs on one sheet as possible.

Once you have a set of designs on regular

Remember what it was like to play with your friends?

You still need that feeling in your life.

You need play in your friendships—for that quality of play is what lifts you, renews you, and refreshes you. You need friends who are willing to play with you—especially friends who like to "go out and play."

How you play together, of course, depends on the interests you share and the diversions that bring you joy. Some friends love to play games such as Scrabble or croquet. Some share physical activity—tennis or racquetball or sailing. Still others love garage-sale excursions or refinishing furniture in the backyard—or just basking on the deck. And some love to share adventures and collect stories for future telling—like the time my friend Yoli and I decided to take her husband's kayak out on the bay. We were not the best and most experienced of rowers, and we spent most of that outing going backward. But when we were through, we pulled the kayak up on the shore and lay down and laughed—restored by our afternoon of playing together and better friends than ever before.

So let's go outside to play. Let's run on the beach and build castles in the sand.

Before that, or afterward, there'll always be time for tea.

What We Owe Our Friends:
> Our loyalty
>
> Our love
>
> Our genuine concern for their well-being

Why We Need Our Friends:
> For fun and companionship
>
> For strength
>
> For insight and identity

Why We Need Our Girlfriends:
> Because we need to talk
>
> Because there are things a man
>   just doesn't "get"

August

CELEBRATING SHARED WORK

A "Job Well Done" Tea

*Verily great grace may go
With a little gift; and precious
are all things that
come from friends.*

—Theocritus, trans. R. C. Trevelyan

Don't you think the term *working woman* is a little redundant? I do. As far as I'm concerned, the word *woman* tells it all!

Most women I know work very hard and accomplish an amazing amount, whether they hold a job outside the home or devote full time to managing a household. Women have been working hard through the centuries—and much of that time they've been working *together*.

Remember pioneer women with their quilting bees and canning parties? Remember the women marching together to promote temperance or votes for women, or Rosie the Riveter working side by side with her sisters to support the war effort in the forties? Today, when more women than ever are working outside the home, productivity experts have noticed that women tend to bring a unique spirit of cooperation and mutual support that really helps get things done.

Almost since the beginning of time, women have been in on the secret that working together, especially with friends we love, is a great way to double the satisfaction and lighten the load. Working side by side adds a special dimension to both the job and to our friendship. And it can add a special dimension as well to the fellowship we enjoy when we gather together afterward to enjoy a cup of tea and congratulate each other on a job well done.

This tea is a perfect way to celebrate the culmination of a long-term project—a seminar completed, a contract signed, or a quilt all ready to auction off. It's a lovely end to a day-long group effort such as a garage sale or a spring-cleaning binge. It's even a nice way to reward yourselves for a morning of working hard at your individual homes. Especially if the work was a little grubby, it feels just delicious to clean up and relax together in late afternoon over a refreshing cup of lemony mint tea.

You might even find yourself and your friends planning work projects together—just so you can enjoy the reward of a "job well done" teatime afterward!

A Simple Setting

If you've been working hard over a paint bucket or a committee project, you probably don't have much time for elaborate decorating—so you want to keep everything about this tea simple as well as lovely. Look for ways to use these ideas with what you already have.

For instance, you can lend your tea table a fresh summery look—and a bit of sixties style—with a summery blue-and-white gingham tablecloth and crockery pitchers full of daisies from the grocery store. (For an even more contemporary look, fill the bottoms of clear glass vases with fresh lemons before adding the water and the flowers.)

Top the table with a square of white linen or Battenburg lace. Napkins can be white and lace-trimmed—old-fashioned hankies look beautiful for this purpose—or blue gingham to match the tablecloth. For napkin rings, use rings cut from toilet paper tubes and daisy appliques from the fabric store. Just paint the tubes white and attach the daisies with hot glue. Simpler still, you can tie the napkins with a length of blue or white ribbon and tuck a fresh daisy in the front of each.

If you are one of those people who collect blue-and-white dishes, this is a lovely opportunity to show them off. You can even garnish your dishes with lemon slices to carry out the blue, white, and yellow color scheme and tuck a few lemons among your jars of daisies to add a touch of the unexpected.

For this simple, satisfying tea, a decorated table and easy, delicious goodies is really all you need, along with the company of your tired but happy friends, of course. If you have a little extra time, however, you can add a touch of whimsy by making simple "pat yourself on the back" favors—the directions are on p. 63. Or you can place a few extra crocks of flowers around the house—a bunch of daisies in your entranceway, a bowl of lemons on the sideboard. A very quick way to say welcome at your door is to tie a big bow on your mailbox or around the neck of a big stuffed animal on a bench. Hang a sign on the door that proclaims "A Job Well Done!" and you'll be ready.

$\mathcal{S}$OMETHING $\mathcal{D}$ELICIOUS

MINTED LEMONADE

This is another cold tea drink, perfectly refreshing for a summer's day. You can also serve it hot—just add hot water instead of cold. You might want to add a little more water because you won't have the ice cubes to dilute it.

> 6 cups boiling water
> ½ cup lightly packed fresh mint leaves
>   or 7 bags of herbal mint tea
> 4 cups cold water
> 2 12-ounce containers of frozen lemonade
>   concentrate

In a teapot, pour boiling water over tea bags; cover and steep 5 minutes. Remove the tea bags. Place frozen lemonade concentrate in a heat-proof pitcher and pour some of the hot mint tea over it; stir until lemonade is thawed. Add the

rest of the mint tea and the cold water. Then pour the mixture into ice-filled glasses and garnish, if desired, with lemon and mint.

EXTRA-EASY CHOCOLATE CHERRY CAKE

If you like chocolate-covered cherries or Black Forest cake, this treat is for you—and the bonus is that it's very, very simple to make. For a special treat, serve each slice with a dollop of real whipped cream and top it with a maraschino cherry. This recipe will serve 15 or more, depending on how you cut the cake.

> nonstick cooking spray
> 1 box chocolate cake mix (enough for two
>   layers, with no pudding in mix)
> 3 eggs, beaten
> 1 can cherry pie filling
> 1 teaspoon almond extract
> 1 cup chopped almonds, divided
> 1 ½ cups semisweet chocolate chips
> maraschino cherries, drained, for garnish

Preheat oven to 350°. Generously spray a 9-by-13-inch cake pan with cooking spray and set aside. Empty cake mix into mixing bowl. Add eggs and extract and stir with wooden spoon until well blended. Carefully blend in pie filling and ¾ cup chopped almonds. Pour into prepared pan and bake at 350° for 30 minutes or until a toothpick inserted in center comes out clean. When you remove the cake from oven, sprinkle the chocolate chips evenly over the top and cover loosely with a piece of waxed paper. Wait 2 or 3 minutes, then use a metal spatula to smooth the melted chocolate over surface of the cake.

Sprinkle rest of almonds over the top and quickly score the chocolate for serving-sized pieces. Place pan on a wire rack to cool completely before you cut the cake.

Something to Make: "JOB WELL DONE" BACK PATTERS

These whimsical favors are a snap to make using stray children's gloves.

Simply choose a small knitted glove or mitten and stuff lightly with polyester fiberfill. Using a yarn needle and several strands of yarn or embroidery floss, sew a simple running stitch around the wrist of the glove. Leave the two ends of yarn hanging.

Next, take a thin strip of wood about twelve inches long and one inch wide—an old ruler, a length of lath or molding, or one of those wooden paint stirrers hardware stores sometimes hand out. Sand the wood lightly and prime it if necessary, then paint with acrylic paints in the colors desired. When it's dry, poke one end deeply into the glove and adjust the fiberfill around it. Run a line of hot glue or all-purpose

Teatime Tidbits

ALTHOUGH TEA ORIGINATED IN CHINA, TRAVELED TO EUROPE WITH THE DUTCH, AND BECAME THE NATIONAL DRINK OF ENGLAND, *ICED* TEA WAS INVENTED IN AMERICA—BY AN ENGLISHMAN WHO LIVED IN CALCUTTA! BUSINESS WAS TERRIBLE FOR RICHARD BLECHYNDEN, WHO WAS SELLING HOT TEA AT THE 1904 LOUISIANA PURCHASE EXHIBITION IN ST. LOUIS. SO THE ENTERPRISING BRIT POURED HIS TEA OVER ICE IN TALL GLASSES AND MADE HISTORY WITH THE REFRESHING BEVERAGE.

craft glue all around the stick right under the yarn stitching, then tighten the two ends of the yarn to close the glove around the stick. Press it against the hot glue to secure. Finish the back patter by tying the yarn tightly, cutting off the loose ends, and tying a bright ribbon over it.

Decorate your glove any way you like with fabric pens or embroidery—add a name, draw on daisies, sew on an applique, or embroider a design. Finally use a paint pen to write the following on the handle: "Give yourself a pat on the back!"

Something to Think About
A Job to Do Together

If you're not in the habit of looking for ways to enjoy the company of friends while you work…well then, that's something to explore. For there's something about working side by side that builds friendships like nothing else can. Working together not only makes the work go easier; it also creates a shared history and helps you get to know each other better. In fact, there's no better way to learn a person's true character than to see her on the job.

Almost any kind of chore—from painting the fence to stuffing envelopes to putting in a new drain—can be accomplished together. Creative endeavors such as decorating a house or designing a publicity plan for the new museum show will almost always profit from the synergy of compatible minds. Motivated friends can even devise ways to share professional tasks—like a freelance writer I know who goes out of her way to procure assignments she can do with her best friend. The two of them live thousands of miles away from each other, but they use the vehicle of shared work to give themselves more time together—sometimes with a tax write-off!

As I see it, there are three basic ways that women can nurture friendships while working together—and I think we should seize every opportunity. First, we can get together to take care of tasks that are dull, repetitive, or daunting—anything from scrubbing floors to addressing Christmas cards. Second, we can step into the breach and help when one person's workload turns into overload—keeping the kids, helping cook and clean, or even answering the phone. Finally, we can use our creativity to search out fun or challenging projects we can do together. Here are just a few ideas for satisfying projects your friends might want to take on as a group:

- *Team up on an unfavorite chore* such as washing windows—do one house a week, then have a party.
- *Cook a monster pot of spaghetti sauce together* and take home in jars for weekday dinners.
- *Bake cookies or fruit bread* and leave them in the teacher's lounge of your children's school.
- *Cook and deliver one day of Meals-on-Wheels.*
- *Volunteer together at a soup kitchen* or a Habitat for Humanity house.
- *Organize a multifamily garage sale*—and clean out your attics and garages.
- *Sponsor and chaperone a kids' field trip.*
- *Set up ironing boards*, pop a great CD in the player, and take care of all your "pressing" concerns.
- *Participate in a fun run* (or walk) for an important cause. Give your group a name and wear matching sun visors or T-shirts.
- *Team teach a class or a Bible study* for a selected period—plan together, then alternate leadership responsibilities.

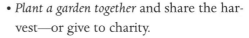

I know that together...we can.

- *Plant a garden together* and share the harvest—or give to charity.
- *Get a craft book and learn to make something new together.*
- *Make a quilt together* and raffle it for a fund-raiser.
- *Spend a morning putting all your photos into albums.*

And when you're all through with your projects, of course, it will be time for a cup of tea. As the delicious aroma swirl around you, you will look into the beloved faces of your friends, sharing the satisfaction of a job well done and the joy of having someone to do it with.

September
CELEBRATING LAUGHTER
A Topsy-Turvy Tea

*We cannot really love anybody
with whom we never laugh.*

—Agnes Repplier

Teas don't have to be stuffy and solemn. Remember Alice and the Mad Hatter? Remember Mary Poppins's tea party on the ceiling? Remember Pooh getting stuck at Rabbit's house after stopping for "a little something"? The history of tea is absolutely full of laughter—that's one reason little girls love tea parties so much!

This is your chance to capture some of that levity for a tea party that's just a little silly but mostly just plain fun. It's a perfect chance to celebrate with your friends who like to laugh—and what treasures those friends are! It's a slightly goofy reminder that life really is serious, but not all *that* serious. In fact, it's a perfect tea to plan for after work, a true "happy hour" that doesn't require any spirits but the spirit of fun.

A topsy-turvy tea takes a little panache to pull off, because the way your guests react will depend a lot on your attitude. It helps to ask one of your craziest friends to cohost—I've found that inspired silliness is easier to pull off when two of you are planning it together.

66

The basic idea behind this kind of tea is to turn the table on expectations. You can start by sending out invitations in the form of thank-you notes. Buy thank-you cards and write them by hand: "Donna, I was so glad you were able to attend my Topsy-Turvy Tea on September 15. It was lovely to see you right there on my doorstep at 5:30 that afternoon, and I really enjoyed our time together. It seems that I always end up laughing when I'm with you! I do hope we can get together again very soon. Love, Emilie. P.S. If you have any questions about this, please call me at (your number)."

When your guests call to find out what's up—believe me, they'll call!—you can give them party details and instructions. For instance, you can ask them to wear something backward or upside down, or to come through the backyard or the garage. It's fun to make the price of admission a good joke—they have to tell one to get in.

When your guests do arrive with their jokes all ready, hand them a silly hat to wear backward. You'll find that hats are great accessories for any party where you need a little bit of highbrow craziness. There's just something about a hat that invites people to act a little differently than normal.

The real fun of a topsy-turvy tea comes from the contrast of formal teatime manners and the unexpected changes in the routine. There are all sorts of ways you can accomplish this. You can have assigned seats and name cards, for instance, and then tell each person to sit at another person's seat. You can have all the guests sit on the floor. Or you can just enjoy your tea with a straight face, letting your topsy-turvy settings—see below—provide the enjoyment.

After tea, there's no limit to what you can do. It might be fun to gather around the VCR and enjoy some classic cartoons, sitcoms, or stand-up comedy routines. By all means, you should tell each other your jokes, perhaps video-taping your "routines." And this is one party where games and activities can really shine. With a box of dress-up clothes, you can improvise costumes and make a video for your kids. You can decorate your hats with feathers and sequins and have a style show. You can put on music and lip synch and dance like your favorite pop stars. And games like Charades are great, but nothing

brings out the topsy-turvy laughs like Twister. Bring it out if you've got the nerve!

By the end of your time together, your party might have gotten a little rowdy and un-tealike. There's nothing really wrong with that if the laughs are heartfelt. As you escort guests to the door, be sure and bid them welcome and wave hello as they leave. And the day after the party, why not send each guest an invitation in the mail with a tiny note at the bottom reminding them that it's a topsy-turvy invitation—in other words, a thank-you note!

A Somewhat Silly Setting

The decorating for your topsy-turvy tea will be very important for setting the mood. The look should begin before the guests ever arrive at your door—with a couple of little touches that just aren't quite *right*. Try a couple of pink flamingos on the front lawn with their backs turned. Hang a "welcome" wreath on your garage door with the garage door opener wired to it. Or deck your front entranceway with a sign that says, "Goodbye. Thanks for coming!"

Once inside, you can use your imagination for little topsy-turvy touches. Try replacing some of your framed family photos with silly portraits of animals or old black-and-whites of movie stars. You could hang a Christmas wreath in the bathroom or arrange a lovely Easter basket on a living room table and stand another flamingo in the corner!

For the tea table itself, you can get a lot of mileage from upside-down place settings—first the turned-over teacup, then the saucer, then perhaps a cake plate, all topped with a little clay pot and a silly-looking edible flower (see directions below)! If you want place cards, make them out of good card stock with the names written in elegant script—next to a hilarious comic strip.

For serving, this is the time to pull out your novelty teapots, unusual plates and bowls, and conversation-piece napkin rings—in the shapes of animals, vegetables, or whatever you can find. A Christmas platter next to a Noah's Ark tea set—with a Star Wars cookie jar decorating the sideboard—might add just the perfect offbeat nuance. To keep the look silly and whimsical (and not tacky), be sure to use your nicest linens, focusing on pleasing colors and composition.

A centerpiece made out of cartoonlike cupcake flowers will complete the decor for your table—and extras serve as refreshments and favors. (The instructions are on p. 72.)

*S*OMETHING *D*ELICIOUS

SILLY AND SWEET FLOWERING CUPCAKES

These instructions will make about 48 mini-cupcakes—about 12 for the centerpiece, 1 per guest for favors, and the rest to serve on a plate as part of the refreshments.

nonstick cooking spray and flour
1 white or yellow cake mix, plus ingredients necessary to mix (such as water and an egg)
1 can ready-made frosting in chocolate or vanilla
assorted candies to make flower designs on cupcakes (candy-coated chocolates, little gumdrops, fruit-shaped candies, hard candies, sliced colored marshmallows)
Spray and flour miniature muffin pans or use

small paper liners (green would work well). Prepare cake mix according to package instructions and bake in muffin cups. (You'll probably need to shorten the baking time, so watch them carefully.) Cool completely on wire racks, then frost each miniature cupcake. Use assorted candies to decorate the tops of cupcakes like silly flowers. Create an assortment of different flower faces.

EGG-ON-YOUR-FACE SANDWICHES WITH TARRAGON

The simplest salad of all gets a new zing from tarragon and Dijon mustard. If you like, you can make these into open-faced sandwiches—cut into rounds

Teatime Tidbits

HANDLES WEREN'T ADDED TO TEACUPS UNTIL ABOUT THE MIDDLE OF THE EIGHTEENTH CENTURY. BEFORE THAT, LADIES AND GENTLEMEN HELD THE HOT CUPS PINCHED BETWEEN THUMB AND FOREFINGER—AND POURED THE TEA INTO SAUCERS TO BE COOLED AND SIPPED.

with cookie cutters and make silly faces with black olives, pickled red-pepper slices, alfalfa sprouts, or whatever you could think of. (In that case, they'd be "Face on Your Egg Sandwiches"—and you can even ask your guests to help decorate!) This recipe makes about 32 sandwiches.

> 4 large hard-cooked eggs, peeled and finely chopped
> ¼ cup mayonnaise, or as needed to mix
> 1 teaspoon Dijon mustard
> 2 teaspoons fresh, chopped tarragon
> 2 teaspoons fresh, chopped chives
> 2 teaspoons pickled red sweet pepper, chopped
> ¼ teaspoon fresh chopped lemon zest
> salt and freshly ground black pepper
> dash of lemon juice or bottled hot pepper sauce, if desired
> 16 slices of fine-textured white or wheat bread
> unsalted butter, softened

Combine eggs, mayonnaise, mustard, herbs, and sweet pepper in bowl; mix well. Season to taste with salt, pepper, lemon juice, or hot sauce. Spread each slice of bread with softened butter. Spread buttered side of half the slices with egg mixture, dividing evenly among the slices. Top with rest of bread slices, buttered side down. Cut the crusts off each sandwich and cut into four fingers.

FUN FRIENDSHIP FACTS

Friendship Day is in September. On September 17, 1997, the national Kappa Delta sorority created a special day for women to celebrate their friendships with one another. The sorority called it National Women's Friendship Day, and it's now regularly celebrated on the third Sunday of September.

Something to Make
A SILLY FLOWER CENTERPIECE AND FAVORS

To make this silly centerpiece, you'll need about 12 Silly and Sweet Flowering Cupcakes, some green ribbon, and a variety of small candies left over from decorating them. You'll be "planting" your cupcakes in a heavy dish with four- to six-inch straight sides—a heavy soufflé dish or a rectangular terracotta planter will work well. In addition, you'll need 12-inch lollipop sticks from a craft store, a block of florist's foam to fit your dish, some strong double-stick tape, a craft knife to cut the foam, and some clean pebbles to help balance the weight of the flowers.

Cut the florist's foam to fit the bottom of your dish but not fill it entirely. Anchor it firmly on the bottom of the dish with double-stick tape. Tie green ribbon in big bows around the lollipop sticks to suggest leaves, then press one end of the lollipop sticks into the bottoms of the cupcake flowers to make stems. Carefully arrange these flowers in the florist's foam. If you like, you can cut them to several different lengths before inserting them in the cupcakes. Don't arrange them too tightly or put in too many; there should be plenty of "air" around each flower. Finally, cover the florist's foam with a layer of clean pebbles or glass pebbles to weight the centerpiece and finish with a layer of hard candies for "soil."

To make an individual favor, you can anchor a single flower in a small terracotta pot. Secure a small block of foam with tape in the bottom of the pot. Cut the lollipop stick to about eight inches. Tie a bow around it, insert in a cupcake, and anchor it in the foam. Fill the pot with pebbles and top with a layer of hard candy for "soil."

Something to Think About
THE GIFT OF
LIGHTHEARTEDNESS

What would you do if you couldn't laugh with your friends? Laughter is surely a healing, restorative part of the fun that comes with friendship. It's laughter that lubricates our irritations, that releases our tensions, that feeds our joy. Whether it comes from gentle teasing or funny anecdotes or cartoons clipped from the paper or just silliness and giggles, it's the laughter that helps keep things warm and joyful even in the midst of pain.

The ability to be silly together adds a special quality to the fun in any friendship. That's because it takes a lot of trust to let down your guard and act a little undignified, even with someone you love. When you feel free to act absolutely goofy with a friend, you understand most fully the freedom a friendship can grant.

Think about it. When was the last time you grabbed a friend and went to the park to swing

or shared impersonations of people you both know or sat down on the floor and colored to your heart's content or bought yourself balloons to carry through the mall. When was the last time you found yourself really giggling?

Count yourself blessed if you have a friend who doesn't mind that kind of silliness or, even better, who wants to do it with you.

For that matter, count yourself blessed for all the fun you have with your friends!

Friends mirror each other. I look at me through your eyes and see someone I like.

October
CELEBRATING MEMORIES
An Herbal Teatime Reunion

When twilight drops her curtain down
And pins it with a star,
Remember that you have a friend
Though she may wander far.

—Lucy Maud Montgomery
Anne of Green Gables

"Keep in touch!"

We've all said it at one time or another to friends who were moving away from us in one way or another—to another city, or to another job, or to another era of life. We've heard it, too, from beloved friends gathered to tell us good-bye. Most people realize instinctively that friendships are precious investments, well worth the time and trouble of maintaining even when time and distance and circumstance alter the relationship.

"Keeping in touch" isn't always easy, though. Cards, letters, phone calls, and e-mails can all help us maintain contact with our dear friends from other times in of our lives, but eventually we find ourselves longing to get together just one more time—to share the common memories that bind us together and the divergent ones that have changed us since those together days.

That, of course, is the reason for reunions. They are times when we pay tribute to the friendships that have made us what we are, even as we nurture and renew the bonds that make keeping in touch worthwhile. The memories we savor together linger and haunt us like the piquant aromas of herbs from the garden and the sweetness of garden flowers. How fitting to organize a reunion of old friends around a theme of herbs and flowers—especially rosemary, the herb that signifies remembrance.

This can be a lovely tea to hold outdoors on a bright blue Indian summer

day. If you are a gardener or have access to a garden, this tea will be especially easy to plan and prepare for, but lacking such a resource, you can find most of what you need at a good florist, an herb farm, a nursery, or even a supermarket.

You don't really need to plan activities. It's very unlikely you'll be at a loss for words with old and dear friends. But a little advance planning can make it even more fun for your guests to reminisce and catch up with each other's lives. Have plenty of photos on hand, plus yearbooks, old letters, and other memorabilia. And don't forget a stereo that plays the "good old songs," whether on vinyl, tape, or CD!

An especially fun idea for a reunion tea is to prepare for each guest a remembrance album—or, if you prefer, an *update* album. Call or write ahead of time to collect information and photos from the time you were together as well as the current time. Then use these resources with your computer or a copy machine to design a page or section for each friend in attendance—and be sure to include her address, phone number, and e-mail address if she has one. Copy a set of all the personal pages for each guest, bind them together into a booklet or scrapbook with a pretty cover, and have them on hand when everyone arrives. They'll be great conversation starters and wonderful mementos of a lovely time of warm herbal tea, warm muffins, and even warmer friendships.

A Memorable Setting

Graduated shades of dusty green—from dark sage up to a light gray-green—will provide a beautiful background for a collection of herbs and fall flowers and a theme of remembrance. Aim for an ambience that recalls a drowsy Tuscany afternoon. Plan on at least three different greens for your table: a dark undercloth, a lighter table topper, a still lighter one for your napkins. If you have them, weathered wooden or iron tables or chairs will add to the ambience. Try overlapping two different-colored square cloths diagonally over such a table, letting the corners remain bare. (This is also a lovely way to dress a buffet or side table.)

Potted herbs of different varieties and different sizes are perfect for a centerpiece. If you plan far enough in advance, you can grow your own—or just contact a good nursery. Choose rosemary, lavender, thyme, lemon verbena—whatever pleases your senses and carries a friendship message—as well as fall-friendly purple pansies, trailing ivy, and other "friendship" flowers. Place them in weathered-looking stone or terracotta containers, group them together in the center of the table, and wind ivory, green, and purple ribbons around and among them. Ivory tapers decked with herbal wreaths will provide a sense of glowing warmth even outdoors; simply hot-glue bunches of herbs to a small wire or grapevine wreath and fit it around the top of the plain glass or wooden candleholder.

Pressed pansies and herbs sandwiched between pairs of identical glass plates can provide a striking and surprising place setting. Add porcelain cups and saucers in a variety of botanical patterns and top off with napkins tied with more of the ribbon, a little bouquet of herbs, and a single flower tucked into each one. Be sure to garnish the serving platters with herbs and flowers and scatter a confetti of herb leaves and blossoms on the tablecloth and even the floor. (Outdoors, a generous sprinkle of herbs underfoot will release an intoxicating aroma just from being trod upon.) For a final touch of herbal loveliness, shape a small heart-shaped rosemary wreath to hang on each chair.

Your garden center or nursery can help you continue your antique herb garden theme throughout the rest of your house. Look for cone-shaped rosemary "trees" or ivy topiaries and wind them with the ribbon for a side table or the patio steps. Wind a banister with ivy or position a piece of garden statuary decked with herbs on the front porch to welcome guests. Pieces of weathered-looking marble statuary or topiary trees will lend an old-world feel to your table, patio, or yard. You can even hang bunches of fragrant dried herbs tied with ribbons in the bathrooms or closets.

Through it all, don't forget that you're holding a reunion. Fill your home with framed photos of all the gathering friends. If you have a group shot from a time you were together, give it a place of honor on your tea table, tucked in among the planters and the ribbons—a testimony that the real center of your celebration is not the herbs and flowers, but the lovely relationships and the happy memories.

Something Delicious

ROSEMARY-CHEDDAR MUFFINS

A savory and delicious twist on a traditional muffin. If you like these, try substituting other herbs such as basil, thyme, or a fines herbes mixture for the rosemary.

 2 cups unsifted all-purpose flour
 2 tablespoons baking powder
 1/2 teaspoon salt
 2 eggs
 2 tablespoons oil
 1 tablespoon honey
 1 cup milk
 2 tablespoons fresh rosemary, chopped
 1/8 teaspoon cayenne or dried mustard
 1/2 cup sharp cheddar, finely shredded

Heat oven to 400°. Grease regular-sized muffin tin with oil or cooking spray or line with paper liners. Sift the dry ingredients together and stir in the cheese and rosemary. In another bowl beat the eggs, then add the oil, honey, and milk. Combine the dry and liquid ingredients and mix just until blended. Pour batter into muffin cups, sprinkle with a little extra cheese, and bake for 25 minutes or until done. Let cool slightly before removing from pan.

LEMON-BLUEBERRY SOUR CREAM CAKE WITH PANSIES

Luscious and lemony and decked with purple pansies to match the purple berries within, this cake will be a star on your tea table. It will serve at least 16 people and probably more.

Teatime Tidbits

HERBAL TEAS ARE REALLY *TISANES* MADE BY INFUSING EDIBLE LEAVES OR SPICES SUCH AS CHAMOMILE, HIBISCUS, OR MINT IN WATER TO MAKE A SOOTHING, DELIGHTFUL, AND OFTEN HEALTHFUL DRINK. TISANES VARY IN PERSONALITY AND COLOR AND ARE MOSTLY CAFFEINE FREE. MANY HAVE MEDICINAL QUALITIES, TOO, AND CAN HELP SOOTHE UPSET STOMACHS, QUIET COUGHS, OR HELP YOU SLEEP. BE SURE TO READ THE LABELS ON YOUR HERBAL TEAS, AND CHECK WITH A NUTRITIONIST OR HEALTH-FOOD STORE IF YOU HAVE ANY QUESTIONS.

3 cups flour

1/4 teaspoon baking soda

1/2 teaspoon salt

1 cup butter, softened

2 tablespoons lemon juice or 2 teaspoons
    lemon extract

grated peel of two lemons

3 cups sugar

6 eggs

1 cup sour cream

2 cups frozen blueberries

2 cups confectioners' sugar

1/2 cup fresh lemon juice

pansies in assorted colors (grown without
    pesticide) to garnish

Preheat oven to 350°. Generously grease and flour a large tube pan. In a medium bowl, sift flour, soda, and salt. Cream the butter in a large mixing bowl; add lemon peel and lemon juice and then gradually add sugar. Beat two minutes. Beat in eggs two at a time, mixing thoroughly after each addition and two to three minutes after all the eggs have been added. Add half the flour and mix on lowest speed until blended. Add all the sour cream, the rest of flour, and mix until smooth. Fold in blueberries. Pour batter into prepared pan, smooth the top, and bake for 60 to 80 minutes. Cool 20 minutes in the pan, then turn onto a cooling rack. After cake is completely cool, mix confectioners' sugar and lemon juice to form a smooth mixture. Drizzle over top of cake to glaze, then decorate edges and top of cake with pansies.

Something to Make:
A WREATH FOR REMEMBRANCE

"As for Rosemary," wrote Sir Thomas More centuries ago, "I lette it runne all over my garden walls, not onlie because my bees love it, but because it is the herb sacred to remembrance and to friendship." This fragrant herb's reminiscent qualities plus its lacy beauty make it a perfect material for concocting these dainty wreaths. Hang one over the edge of each guest's chair for a welcome, then invite guests to take them home and hang them to dry as a fitting remembrance of your time together.

To make these miniature heart-shaped wreaths, you will need some heavy-gauge wire and wire cutters, a roll of silver florist's wire, some scissors, a collection of rosemary branches cut into short sprays, some lengths of satin ribbon in colors of purple, gold, ivory, or green, a glue gun, and some dried or silk pansies to decorate.

Begin your wreath by twisting a length of wire into a six-inch circle. Then, by pinching it at the base and the top, form it into a heart shape. Cut short sprays of rosemary. Beginning at the "dip" at the top of the heart and working around toward the point, wire the sprays to the heart with the florist's wire. Adjust the rosemary needles as you go to conceal the wire—and overlap the base of each new spray with the end of

the previous one. Tie the ribbon to the top to conceal the ends of the first stems. Hot-glue a couple of pansy blossoms onto the center of the ribbon.

Something to Think About
KEEPING IN TOUCH

Distance doesn't always make the heart grow fonder. Old friends do drift away sometimes, and friendships do fade. But good friends can keep their relationship humming long after one or both have said goodbye—and new friendships can even flourish over the long-distance lines. Here are just a few ideas that can help nurture long-distance friendships—or even a whole circle of friends:

- *Invest in Ma Bell.* Think of telephone bills as friendship investments. If money is tight, a separate phone card for "friend calls" can help you stick to your budget.
- *Don't forget to write.* There's just something special about receiving a card or letter in the mailbox—and a card or letter can be reread and treasured for years. If you want to keep a group of friends together, consider a periodic newsletter or a round-robin letter that begins with one friend and is passed along and added to by the others.
- *Go high-tech with faxes and e-mails.* E-mail is an especially handy, immediate, and inexpensive way to keep current with long-distance friends. Some people say it's revitalized their faraway friendships.
- *Send pictures.* Do you have duplicate shots of the same pose? Send one to a friend with a note on the back.

A friendship is one of the few things in your life that you want to grow old.

• *Vacation together.* Meet somewhere between your homes—a hotel, spa, or retreat center—for a week of fun and renewing your friendship. Come alone or bring your families.

• *Work together on a long-distance project.* Planning a college reunion or cosponsoring a child from another country gives you an excuse and a reminder to stay in close touch.

• *At least say hi.* During crazy times when there's really no time to write or even phone, a simple postcard or a five-minute phone call can still keep the lines of communication open.

• *Maintain a tradition.* Send a friendship ball back and forth with tiny trinkets, keep the same greeting card volleying back and forth between you, or enjoy a cup of tea together over the phone.

• *Treasure twin mementos.* Look for two or more identical items— teacups, hankies, cookie jars, or T-shirts—in a gift or antique shop. Keep one and send one to a friend or friends as a constant reminder of the bond between you.

• *Pray for each other.* Always and faithfully.

• *Exchange audiotape messages or videotapes of your homes and families.* Be creative. Read an article out loud to the tape player or get your family involved in a fun video production.

• *Send a friend a subscription or enroll her in an "of the month" club.* The monthly arrival of magazines, fruit, or whatever will bring thoughts of you as well.

November
CELEBRATING STORIES

A "Share Your Treasure" Tea

For where your treasure is,
there will your heart be also.
—The Book of Matthew

Friendships thrive on talk, on the telling of stories. This special autumn tea party offers the opportunity for new friends and old to get to know each other better by sharing a little bit of their hearts and lives.

This tea is another that requires some advance instructions; each guest should be asked to bring a personal heirloom and a story about why that item is special. Stress that treasures don't have to be valuable antiques. A treasure can be a recipe or a worn old toy, a letter, or even just a saying or piece of advice. This tea is

really a kind of show and tell for adults—except that the friends who gather for tea will really be showing and telling about themselves.

For a truly unique invitation, look for miniature "treasure chests" at a discount store or gift shop—or paint papier-mâché boxes from the craft store and top with a piece of costume jewelry glued on the lid. Fill with little treats such as wrapped candies and place your invitation on the top. Pack into shipping boxes and mail to your guests or deliver to their doorstep. You'll be sparking their sense of discovery from the very beginning!

Once your guests arrive, of course, that's when the real fun begins. Set out the various treasures in places of honor on side tables draped in velvet. Once everyone has filled her plate and settled down comfortably, you can begin to share. Allow time for each guest to show her treasure

and tell a story about it—how she came to possess it, why it's precious to her, where it lives in her house, or anything else she wants to say about it. If you like, after everyone has had a turn, you can go around again, for the presentation of treasures is bound to bring other treasures to mind.

When the party is drawing to a close and everyone has shown her treasure, it would be nice for you to end with a little speech or meditation about what a treasure these friends are to you and how much you value each one. Then send each friend home with a jeweled votive as a reminder of the treasure she has in the circle of those who love her.

A Warm and Sparkling Setting

An intriguing blend of natural and glitz sets the mood for this tea. You'll be combining nuts, fruits, little pumpkins, and autumn leaves with shining glass stones, bits of old costume jewelry, and dollops of gold paint. They'll all fit together if you keep the color tones similar—deep, mysterious, and beautiful.

Choose a deep brown, eggplant, or even black to cover your table—if you can find inexpensive lengths of velvet or velour, use them! Over this base, drape a large, fringed, embroidered scarf or add fringe to a square of luxurious tapestry. For a centerpiece, fill a treasure chest or cornucopia with a bounty of unshelled nuts touched with gold (use a gold paint pen), gilt-edged miniature pumpkins or other fruit, gold silk leaves, and—surprise—bits and pieces of sparkly costume jewelry or glass rocks in glowing autumnal colors.

Let this treasure spill out onto the table and spark it with dancing votive candle holders studded with glowing glass. For a similar but more contained look, you can fill a large shallow glass bowl with the same treasure and use it to anchor a grouping of pillar candles in various sizes.

Whichever direction your central decoration takes, continue the theme of natural and sparkling throughout the entire table. A candle at each place in a gleaming votive holder provides a touch of individual spark. Napkin rings could be decorated with bits of costume jewelry or gold silk leaves—or try a beaded ponytail holder for an easy source of sparkle.

Don't forget to provide extra tables where the guests can store their "treasures" while they enjoy their tea. Spread more velvet or velour over cardboard cartons of varying heights to provide a museumlike display.

Don't forget your own treasures when you decorate. This is the perfect occasion to highlight your collection of antique eyeglasses, your grandmother's funeral fan, or your lineup of Swedish Dala horses.

$\mathscr{S}$OMETHING $\mathscr{D}$ELICIOUS

HIDDEN TREASURE COOKIE CUPS

Everyone loves these wonderful candy-cookies—and they're really easy once you get the knack of easing them out of the pan! Each recipe makes about 48 cookies.

nonstick cooking spray
¹/₂ cup miniature chocolate chips
2-ounce package "nut topping" (a mixture of chopped peanuts and pecans, available either in the baking section or with ice cream toppings)
1 18-ounce roll refrigerated sugar cookie or peanut-butter cookie dough, chilled
2 8-ounce packages miniature peanut-butter cups
gold paper muffin liners

Preheat oven to 350°. Spray miniature muffin pans well with cooking spray. In small bowl, mix chocolate chips and nut topping; set aside. Slice off thin pieces of refrigerated dough and roll each slice into a smooth ball about 1 inch in diameter. Place a ball of dough into the bottom of each muffin cup and flatten slightly. Unwrap one of the peanut-butter cups (be sure to remove paper "cup" as well as foil!) and place it carefully in the center of a dough ball; press down carefully until top of candy is even with dough. Repeat for each cookie. For best results, there should still be about ¹/₄ inch space at the top of each muffin cup so the dough can expand without overflowing. (I had best results with muffin pans whose cups are about an inch deep.)

Bake cookies 8–10 minutes, or until cookie dough has puffed up around candy and has begun to brown. Remove pans from oven, sprinkle a little of the nut-chocolate mixture into the well that has formed over each peanut-butter cup, then return pan to oven for a few more minutes to melt chocolate chips and let cookie dough get a little firmer. Remove pans from oven, cover each loosely with a sheet of waxed paper, and let cool on racks *for at least ten minutes* before removing cookie cups from pans. Then run a thin knife around each cookie cup and lift it out carefully to a plate. Let cool completely, then place into gold paper muffin cups to serve.

FUN FRIENDSHIP FACTS

If you've always suspected that friendship is good for the body as well as the soul—you're right! A nine-year study in California found that the death rates among people with lasting relationships—such as good friendships—were markedly lower than those among more isolated people.

THANKSGIVING SANDWICHES

Give thanks for the treasure of your friendships with these different but delicious sandwiches. This recipe makes about 24 sandwiches, with some cranberry sauce left over for Thanksgiving.

> ½ cup sugar
> ½ cup water
> half of a 12-ounce package fresh
>   cranberries
> small jar of orange marmalade
> 8-ounce package cream cheese
> unsweetened butter, softened
> finely chopped walnuts or pecans (optional)
> 1 loaf cinnamon bread or fine-grained
>   whole wheat bread

Mix the sugar and water together in a saucepan and stir to dissolve the sugar. Bring to a boil, add the cranberries, and return to a boil. Boil gently for 10 minutes, stirring occasionally, then remove from heat. Cool completely at room temperature before making sandwich filling.

To prepare sandwiches, first soften cream cheese in a bowl with a wooden spoon. Add 2–3 tablespoons of the cooled cranberry sauce and about a tablespoon of the orange marmalade. Fold very gently into the cream cheese, working toward a marbled effect rather than a complete mixture. Spread all the bread slices thinly with unsweetened butter, then spread half of them with the cream cheese mixture. If you wish, add a sprinkling of chopped walnuts or pecans, then top with remaining bread slices. Trim off crusts with a serrated knife and cut into fingers or triangles. Refrigerate at least an hour before serving to harden the cream cheese.

Something to Make
JEWELED TREASURE VOTIVES

These easy-to-make candleholders will be beautiful decorating your tea table and also make wonderful gifts for your treasured friends. Make them from clear glass votive candle-holders—either straight-sided or rounded—and those little glass stones from the hobby store that are flat on one side. (They're often sold in the floral department to put in vases.) Look for a variety of warm, jeweled tones to cover either clear or colored votives. The only other tool you'll need is a glue gun and glue sticks, besides small candles to burn inside the cups.

To make the votives, begin by washing and drying your votive cup to remove the price tags and any accumulated dust. Heat up the glue gun, then glue a row of glass stones around the bottom of the votive cup. Continue to add glass stones in rows up the side of the holder, varying the colors and staggering the stones from row to row, until you reach the top. The rows of stones should be irregular and interlocked, but try to align those on the top row with edge of the glass. Let the glue harden, add a candle, and your jeweled votive is ready to grace your table!

If you like the effect of these jeweled candle-holders, experiment with different colors of glass and even with other materials. Beach glass,

Teatime Tidbits

KING GEORGE IV OF ENGLAND WAS ONE OF THE FIRST ENGLISH COLLECTORS OF TEAPOTS. TODAY, LOTS OF PEOPLE (LIKE ME!) TREASURE THEIR COLLECTIONS OF BEAUTIFUL TEA THINGS AND ARE ALSO ON THE LOOKOUT FOR JUST ONE MORE SPECIAL CUP, POT, OR TEASPOON.

marbles, bits of tile, and pieces of broken costume jewelry could all add texture and variety—or a simple, one-color scheme could decorate almost any space.

Something to Think About
GIFTS OF FRIENDSHIP

What can you say about someone who gives you the freeing gift of acceptance, the strengthening gift of trust, the relaxing gift of commonality, the courageous gift of truth? The gift of a friend's laughter lightens our load. The gift of tears can wash our spirits clean. And when a friend forgives us—as they often must—our whole lives are gifted with grace! The gift of such friendship really can't be returned except in kind—in other words, the only completely appropriate gift for the friends we treasure is the gift of ourselves. Still, there are times when our hearts long to present our friends with a token of the treasure they have given us—and the exchange of such tokens over time does strengthen and solidify friendship.

What can you give? Here are just a few ideas—little treasures both sentimental and practical for the special friendships that mean so much:

- *A book from your personal library* with your notes in the margins.

- *A family heirloom*—from your family to hers—with a note explaining it.

- *Something to add to her collection* (a bell, a miniature animal, an antique coffee grinder)—or something to start a new one.
- *Personalized stationery* you made yourself.
- *Something that made you laugh* when you saw it in the store or catalog.
- *Supplies for a hobby she wants to try.*
- *A pastel or oil portrait* made from a photo of the two of you.
- *A T-shirt with your pictures on it*—use the copy transfer technique explained on pages 57–58.
- *A mug, a tea bag, and a phone card:* "Let's have tea together over the phone."
- *Something she just loved but reluctantly put down* when you went shopping together.
- *A monogrammed Bible, hymnal, or prayer book.*
- *A handmade gift* you and the children made during the holiday season.
- *A chain of encouraging cards and notes* when she is going through a difficult time.
- *A personalized calendar* featuring pictures of you, her, and your families.
- *A rosebush or tree* planted in her honor in your yard or a public place.
- *A manicure, pedicure, or massage.*
- *A surprise visit* (when you live in different towns).
- *Free baby-sitting* (offer to let all the kids stay with you overnight!).
- *Dinner for her family*—complete with centerpiece, lighted candles, and you as waitress.
- *An oil change or fill-up at the gas station.*

Friendship is a treasure. If you possess even one nugget of the real thing, you're rich.

December
CELEBRATING FAMILY

A Tea for
Your Friends
and Relations

Friends are life's everyday resource,
life's hidden treasure;
if not for the love we get from our own family of friends,
would we have the courage to be quite the way we are?

—Lois Wyse

Your friends are not necessarily your family, and your family are not always your friends—but what a wonderful privilege to have friends who are also related to you!

I certainly consider my husband, Bob, to be my very best friend—and we love to enjoy tea together. My daughter, Jenny, and son, Brad, have grown into the dearest of friends, especially over the past few years. Granddaughter Christine has been my special tea-party buddy almost from birth, but her younger brothers and my nephews have also entered the

ranks of my friends. And that's not even to mention my playmate cousins, my aunts and uncles, and of course my beloved mother, who taught me how to have tea and for many years was my very best friend.

It works the other way, too, of course. Your closest friends are, in a sense, your chosen family—as much a part of you as those who claim you by blood or adoption. You may consider their families yours as well—one big clan bound together by ties of love and loyalty.

To celebrate the wonder of these family-friend relationships—and to help those friendships grow—it's fun to have a special friendship tea together. It's a perfect event to enjoy during the Advent season—a warm, peaceful break from the pre-Christmas hype. But it's appropriate for just about anytime you want to honor your family of "friends and relations."

This is a wonderful opportunity to enjoy what the British call "high tea," which is really a light sit-down meal served between five and six in the evening—early enough to comfortably include children and older friends. Because this will be a sit-down meal enjoyed around the table, you'll need to limit your guest list according to your table space. But there's no rule that says you can't enjoy this tea with just your husband—and no rule that dictates against adding extra tables, each one decorated and set as lovingly as the next, for a real family-sized celebration.

What should you serve at your friends-and-family style tea? High teas typically feature heartier and often more homely fare than teas served earlier in the afternoon. Bread and butter is a staple, while savory dishes like sausage rolls, salads, and chutneys and relishes often accompany a plate of cold cuts and a beautiful salad. Hearty warm breads like crumpets (similar to our English muffins) or pancake-like drop scones are appropriate and delicious, along with fresh fruit, cakes, and other sweets; plenty of warm, strong tea; and extra helpings of warm family feeling.

And although you might not need the most rigid, formal manners with these people you know so well, you still want to show them the same courtesy and respect you would give to strangers in your home. In fact, the whole point of this family-and-friends tea is

to treat the ones you love like honored guests.

By taking the time and trouble to prepare a beautiful, elegant teatime meal for your friends who are family and your family who are friends, you will have the joy and privilege of giving special treatment to the people you love best.

A Family– Style Setting

Because a high tea is really a light meal, your table will need to be set accordingly— with dinnerware and silver placed as you would for a luncheon or dinner. The table decor should be warm and lovely. Even if your house is decked out for the holidays, it's nice to take a break from Christmas decor for this special meal.

Instead of pulling out your Christmas brocade, for instance, try draping the table in a bistro-style checkered tablecloth, a tartan blanket in rich blues and greens, or a fringed paisley shawl swirling with shades of pink, gold, and eggplant. (Try to find an interesting or unusual table cover that picks up the colors in your favorite china.) Instead of pine boughs, pinecones, and poinsettias, you can use a procession of miniature rosebushes or potted mums in little brass planters, painted terracotta pots, or even miniature galvanized washtubs. Instead of Christmas-themed napkins, try pretty fringed dish towels, rich-colored fingertip towels, or antique hankies in colors to match the rest of the table. Slip them through metal napkin rings (you can make your own from craft wire) or just tie them loosely in a knot and set them on top of the place settings.

Don't forget to add some special touches and surprises throughout the house. Purchase a new doormat or flower arrangement for the front entryway or hang a little chalkboard with a loving message. If you've planned tea to treat your immediate family after work and school, try decorating each of their rooms with a little potted plant that matches the tea table—or welcome them home with a cup of tea on a tray that they can enjoy while they're cleaning up and changing clothes.

Be sure to allow time to freshen yourself up as well, so you can treat these people you love with a big dose of you at your best. Change clothes, redo your makeup, enjoy your own refreshing cup of tea. You'll be ready to fully enjoy your special family of friends and relations.

$\mathscr{S}$OMETHING $\mathscr{D}$ELICIOUS

GIRDLE SCONES (SCOT PANCAKES)

The "girdle" in the name actually means "griddle." These traditional Scottish treats are cooked on a griddle or skillet like pancakes but served in a basket, with butter and jam, like regular scones. They make a hearty staple for a family-style high tea.

> 2 cups plain flour
> ¼ teaspoon salt
> 1 teaspoon cream of tartar
> 1 teaspoon baking soda
> 6 tablespoons sugar
> 1 large egg
> 1 ¼ cups buttermilk
> 2 teaspoons melted butter or oil

Heat a griddle or heavy frying pan and brush lightly with oil or butter. Sift together flour, salt, cream of tartar, and baking soda, then stir in sugar. In a separate bowl, mix egg, butter, and about ¾ cup of the buttermilk. Make a well in center of dry ingredients and add egg mixture, stirring and adding more buttermilk as necessary to make a thick, pancake-like batter. Test the griddle by dropping a small amount of batter onto the surface; bubbles should rise to the top in a few seconds if it is the right temperature.

Drop batter by heaping tablespoons onto hot griddle to make three or four scones. If necessary, spread dough with back of spoon into a flattened 3-inch round. Cook scones until tops are bubbling and bottoms are brown, then flip with pancake turner to cook other side. Continue with this process until all scones are cooked. You may need to regrease the pan after each batch. As scones are cooked, wrap them in a tea towel or napkin to keep them warm while you cook others. Serve warm with butter and honey or jam.

SAUSAGE ROLLS

Flaky and savory, these tea-party staples taste like they were created in a professional bakery—but they're extremely easy to make. Their secret? Frozen puff pastry! This recipe will make about 35 sausage rolls.

> 1 package (17-ounce) frozen puff pastry sheets
> 1 pound bulk pork sausage

Separate the two sheets of pastry in the package, wrap each one in plastic wrap, and thaw both at room temperature for half an hour. Meanwhile, heat the oven to 400°. Leave one package in the refrigerator while you work with other package. Unfold the pastry on a lightly floured surface and carefully roll it into a rectangle measuring about 10 by 12 inches, then cut the rectangle into three strips along fold marks. Take half of the sausage and divide it into thirds (1/6 of the total amount of sausage). Roll each portion into a cylinder the length of a pastry strip. Place it along the long edge of one strip and roll up in pastry. Moisten the edges and press together to seal. Cut each roll into six 2-inch slices, and cut two small diagonal slashes in the top of each with a sharp knife. Place the slices on a baking sheet with the "seam"

down. Bake about 30 minutes or until the pastry is golden and the sausage is cooked through. Repeat with other pastry sheet.

Something to Make
A Decoupage Serving Tray

If you have lots of friends and relations, you probably have a big collection of beautiful cards they've given you and gorgeous pieces of wrapping paper you just can't bear to throw away. You can put these precious pieces of memorabilia to beautiful use by making them part of a one-of-a-kind tea tray.

To do this project, you'll need a tray of some sort—papier-mâché, finished or unfinished wood, even an old metal TV tray. (You'll have to adjust your materials and techniques just a bit for each surface.) You'll also need a sealant and paint appropriate to your surface, some small scissors, several foam brushes, and a jar of decoupage medium from the craft store. (Decoupage medium, which goes by several different names, is a combination of glue and clear finish.) Finally, and most important, you'll need your cards, gift wrap, or whatever paper decorations you want. If you don't want to use cards or gift wrap, you can use color photocopies, old calendars or sheet music, or even fabric and lace. Pictures from magazines and catalogs might also work if the paper is substantial—thinner magazine papers tend to wrinkle badly and show through designs from the back of the paper.

Before you can apply your designs, you'll need to seal the surface. An unfinished wooden tray needs a light sanding (brush off the dust carefully) and a coat of wood sealant. For a metal tray, remove

any rust with steel wool and spray with a rust-proof sealer. Any all-purpose sealer will work for a cardboard or papier-mâché tray. When you've sealed the surface of the tray, color it with a paint appropriate to the surface. When the paint is dry, you're ready to apply the decoration to your tray.

Cut out the designs you want with scissors, angling the scissors slightly toward the picture as you cut. (This creates a beveled edge that adheres more tightly.) Experiment with their arrangement on the tray until you have an effect you like. (You might want to sketch it out on a piece of paper to help you remember.) Then you're ready to apply it to your tray.

First, dip your paper designs in water to relax

the fiber and reduce wrinkles. Then use a foam brush to coat the back of each liberally with decoupage mixture. Brush decoupage medium thinly over the area of the tray where each picture will go, lay the picture on the surface, and smooth it into place with your fingers, gently working out any wrinkles, bubbles, or excess decoupage medium. Continue placing the designs in this manner until all the pieces of your design have been applied to the surface of the tray. Depending on the effect you want, you can overlap the pictures or let a lot of the painted surface show.

When you've finished with the design, cover the entire surface of the tray with three or four coats of the decoupage medium, allowing the tray to dry completely between each coat. For a smoother surface, brush only in one direction and sand the tray lightly between coats of decoupage medium. Finish by sealing the entire surface, front and back, with a clear acrylic sealer.

Something to Think About
A FRIEND YOU ALREADY HAVE

Can a friend be a sister? Or a mother or daughter? What about a colleague or a teacher or the woman who grooms your dog? What about a husband?

I think you know the answer to those questions!

One of the most beautiful things about friendship is that it can transcend categories and roles. In fact, you never know when a person wearing one name tag in your life—mother, sister, neighbor, child's teacher, pastor's wife, casual acquaintance—might step over the labels and sign up as a treasured friend of the heart.

Does this always happen?

You already know this answer, too.

There is a mystery to the ways of friendship. Even when two people are willing, friendship doesn't always blossom. Still, when we see a door to friendship open with someone who is already in our lives, we miss a lot by not stepping through.

After all, finding a friend is like discovering a treasure.

Finding a friend in someone you already love is like finding a treasure in the rafters of your own attic—one of life's most joyful surprises.

Time spent with your family of friends is one of best investments you can make!